WHAT ARE THEY SAYING ABOUT
LUKE AND ACTS?

What Are They Saying About Luke and Acts?

A Theology of The Faithful God

**by
Robert J. Karris, O.F.M.**

PAULIST PRESS
New York/Ramsey/Toronto

Library of Congress
Catalog Card Number: 79-83899

ISBN:0-8091-2191-3

Published by Paulist Press
Editorial Office: 1865 Broadway, New York, N.Y. 10023
Business Office: 545 Island Road, Ramsey, N.J. 07446

Printed and bound in the
United States of America

Contents

For
Hank and Barbara

Preface

For the past six years I have been studying Luke-Acts with great industry. My reading has been extensive and in many languages; my consultation with colleagues has been broad and ecumenical. But while it is important for my readers to know that they are touring Luke-Acts at the hands of a competent guide, it may be of far more significance that they know that in October 1976 I lost my only sister Joanne to cancer. She was beautiful, very bright, and thirty.

My sister's terminal cancer, her death, and the aftermath of that loss have been creative of much human growth and have given me a real-life vantage point from which to view Luke-Acts. I now know more deeply that God is a faithful God, a God of surprises, that out of suffering comes growth, that prayer is the search to decipher God's handwriting—sometimes a handwriting that writes straight with crooked lines—that the love and support of friends and community enable trust, that gratitude is the posture to turn toward the past.

This book, then, is more than a series of benchmarks on the current status of Lukan scholarship. Its subtitle, A Theology of The Faithful God, suggests that it is a creative formulation of a theology of Luke-Acts, a formulation which has been tried in the fire of life. Toward the end of most every chapter, straightforward reporting of Luke's theology will fade into the background, and personal faith reflections will occupy center stage. I write in this vein because I am an artist as well as Scripture scholar, because I am convinced that often what is most personally true is also universally true, and because I sincerely believe that readers want to know more about their communication partner than the usual author's blurb which charts chronological age and academic prowess.

Many groups have contributed to the making of this book. I single out for special mention the following: the Mercy Sisters of College Misericordia, Dallas, Pennsylvania and the participants at their 1977 Summer Scripture Institute; a seminar of twenty priests, religious and lay people from the diocese of Paterson, New Jersey who studied Luke-Acts with me for a week in March 1978; some twenty-five students who worked through Luke-Acts with me during a course in the spring of 1978 at Catholic Theological Union; the participants at the Third Annual Scripture Institute, August 1978, at Bergamo Center, Dayton, Ohio. I owe these people and many others a profound debt of gratitude for their support and insights.

A few technical points. Unless otherwise noted, translations of biblical passages are based on the Revised Standard Version. Footnotes have been eliminated in favor of a bibliographical note in brackets in the body of the text. When the name only of an author is given, full bibliographical data on that author's work will be found at the end of the book in the section entitled "Select Bibliography."

Finally, I express my profound gratitude to Sister Marie McCarthy, S.P. for her expert assistance in the preparation of this book for publication.

1
How To Approach Luke-Acts

Approaching Luke-Acts might be compared to encountering Chicago's O'Hare Airport for the first time. I recall my first experience at O'Hare—so many terminals, ticket counters, gates, and thousands of people milling about. I had to pause, narrow my focus to the ticket counter of the airline I was flying, and ask people for assistance.

Before beginning our journey through Luke-Acts, we pause and get our bearings. We plan to travel through the fifty-two chapters which comprise the two-part volume Luke wrote: The Gospel of St. Luke and Acts of the Apostles. We will ask assistance of those who have traveled this way before.

Or to change the image, we come to Luke-Acts like art students. We ask our instructor to teach us how to see, how to put an entire work of art into perspective, how to spot the characteristics of a particular artist.

In what follows I will first alert you to snippet-itis, a weakness we all have. After that I will introduce you to Luke the artist. Finally, I will advise you that our tour of Luke-Acts is a search and growth operation.

I. Snippet-itis —
A Callus, a Blurring of Vision

Almost all of us have become accustomed to hearing or reading the Scriptures in snippets. The daily and Sunday readings at liturgy give us snippets of an entire work. We hear of a parable, a miracle story, Paul's admonitions to a particular church. Listening to the Scriptures in this way can easily give rise to the weakness of snippet-itis, which prevents us from seeing how the snippet fits into the entire work. Snippet-itis is like a callus on a toe which impedes our fast and comfortable movement, like a blurring of vision which reduces comprehension of the total picture.

In Chapter 2 I will have more to say about the big picture of Luke-Acts. For now, it suffices that both you and I realize that we suffer from the callus of snippet-itis, that we have a tendency to view Luke-Acts like so many unconnected building blocks.

II. Luke the Artist

According to some scholars Luke suffers from muddleheadedness; he does not seem to be in control of his material. For example, he can teach abandonment of all possessions in one place while teaching abandonment of only fifty percent in another place. He can teach that the Lord is returning imminently in one place while in another he insists that the Lord is taking his time in returning.

To me Luke is anything but muddleheaded. But he does not seem to think linearly, in a straight line, with point one following immediately upon point two on a scale of ten. His thought is spiral, spherical, artistic. As he circles the truth, point one may be followed by ten which in turn is followed by eight and then two. On a sphere there are many ways of approaching the center. As you think of your spherical Christmas tree ornaments, recall that the dictionary defines a sphere as "a round body whose surface is at all points equidistant from the center." Recall what we often say about the artist in our midst: "Don't mind him. He's in his own world. He's an artist!"

Luke is like an alert, elderly statesman in a community. He may seem to ramble on, circling the truth, narrowing the distance from the sphere's center with each passing story, proverb or admonition. That elderly statesman follows "Love your family dearly" with "Don't work for your relatives." In answer to the question, "What's the best time of life?" he replies: "The epitome of life is found in the first years of marriage" and "Life is most fresh and meaningful after you recover from a long illness." He says that what gives people the greatest delight also causes them the greatest sadness—love. When we associate with a person like Luke who thinks spherically, it is inappropriate to apply the criteria of linear thinking and insist: "But what is the *true* way of approaching the center?"

We may contemplate Luke the artist and his masterpiece Luke-Acts through the eyes created by a poem written by Sister Mary Catherine Keene, S.P.:

I wander—yes *I*—
   I *do* wander
            in and out
                  of the countries
                        of my person
         speaking
            the language
                  of each new place
      and
         adjusting
            to the mode of travel there
         marveling
            at the strangeness
               between one and another
         marveling
            at the truth:
                  all this is "I"
            reflective
               wandering
                  "Little Inside"
               Known and Knowing
                     Polyform
                     transparency
                     multi-faceted
      and
         so un-utterably
               ONE.

III. Search and Growth Operation

As you explore Luke-Acts, you are going to garner packets of information. You will be able to repeat what you have learned—in a classroom, in a discussion group, on a test, to an interested party. And as you collect these bits of information, you will grow in knowledge.

But exploring Luke-Acts can be more than a data-gathering process. It can also be a search and growth operation. In searching through Luke-Acts we are not going to be led to a formula secreted in some safe-deposit box, so that once we have this formula, we can straight off comprehend the meaning of all fifty-two chapters of Luke-Acts.

Searching through Luke-Acts is more like the searching involved in friendships. The more we get to know another person, the more we realize the mystery, the inexhaustible intelligibility, of that person. Searching through and deepening the relationship leads to deeper love and personal growth. And in loving and growing, we learn more about the other and about ourselves. We search and we grow. The more we search through Luke-Acts, the more we will grow as we are captivated and led forward by Luke's visions of life, Jesus, God, and community.

So we begin the process of this book. In Chapter 2 I will present some remedies for the callus of snippet-itis. Chapter 3 will detail Luke's situation and give some additional insights into his person. In Chapters 4-8 I will direct a search and growth operation on the mysteries of God, Jesus, prayer, poor and rich, and Spirit. The final chapter will capture the vision of Luke and project it for our times. The vision is that of "The Faithful God."

2
Luke-Acts—
The Continuation
of Biblical History

In trying to get some relief from the callus of snippet-itis and to see the big picture of Luke-Acts, we will travel through four areas of consideration. The first section on biblical history will situate Luke-Acts within the various writings which comprise the Scriptures. In the second section we will present a preliminary map of the terrain of Luke-Acts. Section three will scout Luke's purpose by asking questions about beginnings and endings. We will dedicate section four to the theme of hope as a backdrop for understanding Luke-Acts. The perceptive reader will notice that each one of these sections prepares for later chapters of this book, especially for Chapter 3 which treats of Luke's person and his situation. This chapter is like act one of a multi-act play; it announces themes which will be developed at greater length in a subsequent act.

I. What Is Biblical History?

A. What Is History?

Luke-Acts fits into the category of biblical history. That is, it continues the history of God's dealings with his people. And like all history, it is an interpretation of events and not a chronicle which details fact after fact without any prioritizing of them, without giving them any interpretation. To prime the pump for appreciating that the stuff of history writing is events interpreted, I present two accounts of the same "event":

Account One: At 5 P.M. on July 4 a cameraman for Channel 104 set up his camera in the middle aisle of the seating section of the Orchard Park Bandshell. He did not tape to the asphalt the black cables leading from the TV truck to the camera. A couple of times people tripped on the loose cables. At 5:32 P.M. an elderly lady was walking by, holding the hands of two young children. Her feet got tangled in the loose cables. She fell heavily to the asphalt. At 5:39 P.M. the TV cameraman came and taped the loose cables to the asphalt. At 5:47 P.M. an ambulance arrived and took the moaning woman to a nearby hospital.

Account Two: At 5 P.M. yesterday a TV cameraman pushed through a crowd in the seating area of the Orchard Park Bandshell, muttering to himself as he played out his black cables. He had had other plans for the holiday evening. He was so absorbed in his anger that he didn't even notice that a number of people had tripped over his loose TV cables. When informed that an elderly lady had tripped on his cables and fallen heavily to the asphalt, he replied angrily: "Couldn't they see the cables? It's broad daylight." In his anger he had failed to take the normal precaution of taping his black TV cables to the black asphalt. A senior citizen suffers with a broken hip today, the innocent victim of anger. When will we humans ever learn that anger destroys!

With its specification of exact times, the first account approximates a chronicle of the event of the elderly lady's fall. The second account interprets that same event as the result of anger. Luke-Acts is like the second account as Luke interprets the events of the life of Jesus and the Christian community.

Or to use an example closer to home, who of us presents a chronicle account of our family tree? By leaving our skeletons in the family closet, we interpret events in the history of our family. As a matter of fact, if we did not interpret the events of our family history, we would bore all to sleep with the endless recounting of fact after fact after fact. As Luke presents the family history of Jesus and the Christian community, he interprets the facts.

B. *Examples of Biblical History*

To help us appreciate what Luke is after in his biblical history, we select two examples from the biblical history of God's dealings with his people called 1 and 2 Kings. In the first example the biblical historian interprets all the events of Manasseh's lengthy fifty-five year reign in Jerusalem from one main perspective, that of apostasy:

Manasseh was twelve years old when he began to reign, and he reigned fifty-five years in Jerusalem. His mother's name was Hephzibah. And he did what was evil in the sight of the Lord, according to the abominable practices of the nations whom the Lord drove out before the people of Israel. . . . And the graven image of Asherah that he had made he set in the house of which the Lord said to David and to Solomon his son, "In this house, and in Jerusalem, which I have chosen out of all the tribes of Israel, I will put my name for ever; and I will not cause the feet of Israel to wander any more out of the land which I gave to their fathers, if only they will be careful to do according to all that I have commanded them, and according to all the law that my servant Moses commanded them." But they did not listen, and Manasseh seduced them to do more evil than the nations had done whom the Lord destroyed before the people of Israel. And the Lord said by his servants the prophets, "Because Manasseh king of Judah has committed these abominations . . . I will wipe Jerusalem as one wipes a dish, wiping it and turning it upside down. And I will cast off the remnant of my heritage, and give them into the hand of their enemies. . . . Now the rest of the acts of Manasseh, and all that he did, and the sin that he committed, are they not written in the Book of the Chronicles of the Kings of Judah? And Manasseh slept with his fathers, and was buried in the garden of his house, in the garden of Uzza; and Amon his son reigned in his stead (2 Kings 21:1-18).

In the second example a later author updates Solomon's prayer at the dedication of the first temple. In so doing, he tempers a judgment like the one leveled against Manasseh and Judah. He holds out hope for God's people in exile:

When thy people Israel are defeated before the enemy because they have sinned against thee, if they turn again to thee, and acknowledge thy name, and pray and make supplication to thee in this house; then hear thou in heaven, and forgive the sin of thy people Israel, and bring them again to the land thou gavest to their fathers (1 Kings 8:33-34).

Luke-Acts is like these two examples of biblical history. Like the author of the story of King Manasseh, Luke interprets events from one main perspective. Like the redactor of Solomon's prayer, he updates traditions he has inherited and then hands them on to a new generation of believers.

C. Why Does Luke Write Biblical History?

Luke writes Luke-Acts, which is the continuation of the history of God's dealings with his people, to show how Jesus and the Christian community fit into that history. To achieve this goal, Luke relies heavily on one schema, that of promise and fulfillment. From this perspective Acts is not the work of someone who is concerned with the delay of Jesus' parousia (see Conzelmann). Acts is primarily Luke's way of showing how Jesus fulfills the promise that the Messiah brings salvation for all nations. The Gospel is Luke's way of showing how God has been faithful to his promises, for Jesus is proof incarnate of God's fidelity to his promises.

In Chapter 3 we will have occasion to offer more detail on Luke's reasons for writing biblical history. Suffice it for the present that we have located Luke-Acts in the biblical history section of the library which is the Bible.

*II. A Preliminary Map
    of the Terrain of Luke-Acts*

A. An Outline of Luke-Acts

Snippet-itis might give us the impression that Luke-Acts consists of brightly colored strings laid out side by side, but not woven into the unity of a rich tapestry. A brief outline will suggest how connected Luke-Acts really is:

Luke 1:1-4   Luke announces his intention for writing both the Gospel and Acts.

Luke 1:5—2:52   A theme is struck: In Jesus Christ God fulfills his promises to his faithful people.

Luke 3:1—9:50   The Galilean phase of the ministry of Jesus, the fulfillment of God's promises.

Luke 9:51—19:44   Jesus, God's fidelity personified, travels to Jerusalem, gathering disciples around him, challenging all with his teachings, and being rejected.

Luke 19:45—23:56   In Jerusalem, that symbol of God's presence among his people, Jesus is rejected by the Jewish leaders.

Luke 24   The rejected Jesus is accepted by God in the resurrection; Jesus promises the gift of the Spirit and forgiveness of sins in his name for all.

Acts 1:1—2:13	Jesus is faithful to his promises and sends the promised Holy Spirit from the Father. Acts 1:8 sets the tone: God's promises are for all.
Acts 2:14—8:3	Gathering of repentant Jewish people who heed the preaching about Jesus, the fulfillment of God's promises.
Acts 8:4—9:43	Because of persecution the message about Jesus is carried to half-Jews, the Samaritans.
Acts 10:1—28:31	The Gospel is for all people, to the end of the earth; Paul is the prime example of the missionary preacher.

In what follows I will flesh out this skeletal outline by singling out certain points for further comment: fulfillment of promises, rejection theme, and Luke's literary skill.

B. *The Theme of Fulfillment of Promises*

Luke 1:5—2:52 is replete with references to how Jesus' birth is the fulfillment of promise.

Mary's song of praise, her Magnificat, interprets what God has done for her as a fulfillment of God's promises: "He has helped his servant Israel, in remembrance of his mercy, as he spoke to our fathers, to Abraham and to his posterity for ever" (1:54-55). Simeon and Anna are fine examples of the pious Jews who wait upon the Lord to fulfill his promises. Simeon was "righteous and devout, looking for the consolation of Israel" (2:25). Anna "gave thanks to God, and spoke of him (Jesus) to all who were looking for the redemption of Jerusalem" (2:38). For people like Mary, Simeon, and Anna, God can fulfill his promises because they are ready to be surprised by God, who exalts those of low degree (1:52).

Jesus' entire ministry bears the stamp of fulfillment of promise. Luke 4:16-30, especially 4:16-21, opens up a wide window on the meaning of Jesus' ministry. Indeed, the Scripture has been fulfilled which reads: "The Spirit of the Lord is upon me, because he has anointed me to preach good news to the poor. He has sent me to proclaim release to the captives and recovering of sight to the blind, to set at liberty those who are oppressed, to proclaim the acceptable year of the Lord" (Luke 4:18-19).

Luke 24:46-49 contains Luke's theology of fulfillment of promise in a nutshell: "And (Jesus) said to them, 'Thus it is written, that the Christ should suffer and on the third day rise from the dead, and that repentance and forgiveness of sins should be preached in his name to all nations, beginning from Jerusalem. You are witnesses of these things. And behold, I send the promise of my Father upon you; but stay in the city, until you are clothed with power from on high.' " If forgiveness of sins is not preached to all nations, then Jesus would not be the Messiah, then the Scriptures would not be fulfilled on this point. But as Luke shows in Acts, Jesus is the Messiah because forgiveness of sins in his name is preached to all nations. Put another way, Acts is Luke's way of showing to his communities and to their Jewish opponents that Jesus is truly the Messiah because he fulfills that Scripture which says that the Messiah proclaims forgiveness of sins for all nations. Acts is not an afterthought for Luke, but his way of showing how Jesus and the Christian community fit into God's prior dealings with his people.

Chapter 4 will build upon these initial observations on the theme of fulfillment of promise.

C. The Theme of Rejection

The theme of rejection is a rich vein in Luke-Acts. It is detected as early as Luke 2:34-35: "And Simeon blessed them and said to Mary his mother, 'Behold, this child is set for the fall and rising of many in Israel, and for a sign that is spoken against (and a sword will pierce through your own soul also), that thoughts out of many hearts may be revealed." Rejection as well as acceptance greets Jesus in his ministry, as can be seen from the response he receives for his programmatic sermon in the synagogue at Nazareth: "When they heard this, all in the synagogue were filled with wrath. And they rose up and put him out of the city, and led him to the brow of the hill on which their city was built, that they might throw him down headlong" (Luke 4:28-29).

The theme of rejection helps unite the disparate materials which form that unique creation of Luke —the travel narrative (Luke 9:51—19:44). As Jesus moves to Jerusalem to fulfill God's plan for him, he instructs his disciples on the meaning of following in his footsteps, challenges the crowds to convert, and experiences rejection at the hands of the Pharisees/ lawyers.

Luke uses his theme of rejection to show that the Jewish leaders, not the people, were responsible for Jesus' death. The following passage from his passion account is representative of his careful separation of the people from their rulers: "And the people stood by, watching; but the rulers scoffed at him, saying, 'He saved others; let him save himself, if he is the Christ of God, his Chosen One!' " (23:35).

The theme of rejection also pervades Acts. The apostles preach repentance in Jesus' name and give the Jewish people another chance to convert. Three thousand Jews in Jerusalem convert at Pentecost and form the nucleus of the repentant Israel (see Acts 2:41). When Paul preaches, some Jews are invariably converted, but the majority reject his message. As a consequence Paul moves to the Gentiles: "And Paul and Barnabas spoke boldly, saying, 'It

was necessary that the word of God should be spoken first to you. Since you thrust it from you, and
judge yourselves unworthy of eternal life, behold,
we turn to the Gentiles' " (Acts 13:46).

D. *Luke's Literary Skill*

Entire works have been dedicated to describing
Luke's literary skill and artistry (see Talbert, *Literary Patterns*). We confine our remarks to the
speeches/sermons in Acts. Luke has largely composed these speeches, which comprise about thirty
percent of Acts, from traditional materials. Like a
good historian, Luke uses his speeches to interpret
events. But he also uses the speeches for two other
purposes: to announce future events within the
story and to preach to his communities. For example, Peter's speech in Acts 2:14-40 interprets the
event of Pentecost as the activity of Jesus: "Being
therefore exalted at the right hand of God, and having received from the Father the promise of the
Holy Spirit, he has poured out this which you see
and hear" (2:33). In 2:19 Peter announces what is
going to happen next in Acts by stating that the
prophecy of Joel is being fulfilled at Pentecost:
there will be "signs on the earth beneath." Chapter
3 will recount the first "sign" of healing performed
in Jesus' name. Luke also uses Peter's speech in
Chapter 2 to preach to his communities about God's
gracious design in the event of Pentecost; he en-

courages them that God and Jesus are faithful to their promises.

We highlight Luke's literary skill in his use of the speeches of Acts with two further examples. First, Peter's sermon in 2:14-40 is paralleled by Paul's sermon in Acts 13:16-41. This is Luke's way of saying that Paul preaches the same message as Peter does. It is also his way of linking parts of Acts together. Secondly, one searches the latter part of Acts in vain to find more than three examples of the content of Paul's preaching. Luke is mainly content to abbreviate: "Now at Iconium they (Paul and Barnabas) entered together into the Jewish synagogue, and so spoke that a great company believed, both of Jews and of Greeks" (Acts 14:1). Luke attributes three full-blown sermons to Paul: Acts 13:16-41; 17:22-31; 20:18-35. These three sermons are typical of the ones which Paul would preach to Jews (13:16-41), pagans (17:22-31), and Christians (20:18-35).

III. Beginnings and Endings

A. Introduction

As we probe into the depths of Luke-Acts as the continuation of the history of God's dealings with his people, it is important to ask: How does Luke begin and end the two parts of his one-volume work? Answers to this question will be highly revelatory of Luke's purpose.

But before hitting the trail to find an immediate answer to this question, let's pause and plot out our course by reflecting upon the beginnings and endings of books. Have you ever begun reading a spy story in the middle? The spy story just didn't seem to make sense when you entered into its plot on page 150. If one skips the beginning of a book, trying to read the rest of the book may be like trying to powder cork. It's a frustrating task at best.

A story hangs from its ending. Recall the function of the punch line of jokes. The lousy joke teller botches up the joke by mistelling the punch line. Sometimes we peek at the last pages of a mystery story. Once we know that the butler did it, the whole story hangs together. But a fine piece of literature not only hangs from its ending, so that we can look back over the story line and appreciate it more deeply. Its ending points us toward *our* future; it challenges our present and asks how we are to live our futures. In this connection I recall reading the novel *Mortal Friends* by James Carroll. In this work of art Carroll tells the story of Colman Brady who suffered from the modern Midas touch. Every person that Brady touched turned to gold—brilliant, sparkling, but dead. The story ended with Brady's resolve not to gild his grandson with the suffocating gold of possessive love. Truly, *Mortal Friends* hung from its ending. But its story challenged my present and compelled me to imagine my future. For days I meditated, not on Colman Brady's possessive love, but on whether I might be suffocating those I love by possessiveness.

B. Luke 1:1-4

Having imagined ourselves into a favorable position to answer the question about the beginnings and endings of Luke-Acts, let's look at the beginning of the Gospel. We recall that Luke 1:1-4 forms the beginning not only of the Gospel, but also of Acts. I use my own translation which is heavily indebted to the Jerusalem Bible:

Seeing that many others have undertaken to draw up accounts of the events that *have been fulfilled among us*, exactly as these were handed down to us by those who from the outset were eyewitnesses and ministers of the word. I in my turn, after carefully going over the whole story from the beginning, have decided to write an ordered account for you, Theophilus, so that your Excellency may learn how *well founded* the teaching is that you have received.

I have italicized the most important words of this preface Luke addresses to those communities of Christians represented by noble Theophilus. Luke's account in Luke-Acts concerns how God *has fulfilled* his promises. But more important for our present purposes is Luke's concern to show how *well founded* the teaching is. Although there may be evidence that Luke is combating heretics who want to win over Theophilus and family to their side (see Talbert, *Luke and the Gnostics*), it seems that

Luke's main concern in Luke-Acts is to strengthen and console his readers. It remains to be seen from the rest of Luke-Acts and from Chapter 3 why Luke's communities must be encouraged.

C. *Luke 24 and Acts 1:8*

The following points on Luke 24 will suffice. The crucifixion of Jesus is not the end of the Jesus story. Nor does despair wash his disciples off the scene. The Faithful God has raised the hope-filled Jesus from the dead. The crucified and raised Jesus is the Messiah because, as Acts will detail, his apostles preach forgiveness of sins in his name to all nations.

Rather than show how all of Acts 1 knits the Gospel and Acts together, we spotlight Acts 1:8. This verse is vital as the overture to Acts: "And you shall be my witnesses in Jerusalem and in all Judea and Samaria and to the end of the earth." The story line of the rest of Acts follows the fulfillment of promise contained in Acts 1:8.

D. *Acts 28*

The ending of Luke-Acts is very puzzling. Why does Luke end his two-part work with: "And Paul lived there (in his Roman lodgings) two whole years at his own expense, and welcomed all who came to him, preaching the kingdom of God and teaching about the Lord Jesus Christ quite openly and un-hindered" (28:30-31)? It is clear from passages like Acts 20:22-23 and 21:11 that Luke knows of Paul's death. Why doesn't Luke conclude Acts with an account of Paul's martyrdom in Rome? In a word, how does Luke-Acts hang from its ending?

We can arrive at a partial reason for the strange ending of Luke-Acts by exploring some of the im-plications of the fact that Luke wrote biblical his-tory. The figures in biblical history function on a number of levels. For example, David was the greatest of Israel's kings and was used by biblical historians as a symbol and standard by which they could judge the merits of subsequent kings. David was also weak and sinful and thus could function as a symbol of the gratuity of God's grace and forgive-ness. Luke concludes Luke-Acts by using Paul as a powerful symbol for his communities. The Christian God is trustworthy since he stands behind Paul who is able to preach safely and fearlessly in fulfillment of the promise found in Luke 21:15: "I will give you a mouth and wisdom, which none of your adver-saries will be able to withstand or contradict." Be-cause of the sterling example of the persecuted Paul, Luke's communities are encouraged in their defense before Jews of the continuity between Jesus and the traditional Jewish expectation of the king-dom of God. In the person of Paul they find consola-tion in their difficult mission to the Jews, for some Jews do convert (see Acts 28:24). Put in capsule form, Luke ends Luke-Acts with the picture of Paul who is the supreme model of God's fidelity to his promises, the prime example of a person of hope, the exemplar of how Luke's communities should conduct their mission. Luke's communities are indeed consoled, encouraged, and supported in their faith by the example of Paul. For more detail I refer the reader to Chapter 3.

IV. Hope as a Backdrop

We have become so accustomed to reading the stories in the Bible from the perspective of hope that we oftentimes do not consciously avert to that perspective. Just think if the opposite were the case, namely, that the backdrop of Luke-Acts is that of despair. Jesus' "Father, into your hands I commit my spirit" would not be answered by the resurrection, but by silence. Paul's waiting in a Roman prison would be like being put on perpetual telephone hold.

I would compare reading Luke-Acts without the background of hope to the experience I have sometimes had of driving back to Chicago late at night from the western suburbs. When I drove out of the city on the expressway during rush hour, hundreds of cars encircled me. As I returned, there were so few cars that I almost got lost. Gone was the backdrop of hundreds of cars. Mine was the eerie experience of trying to maneuver without the usual landmarks. Without hope as the backdrop, the story of Luke-Acts makes little sense.

I sum up this chapter and point ahead to the

next chapter in this way. The biblical history which is Luke-Acts has as one of its main purposes to show the communities of Theophiluses that the God-faithful-to-promises is a gracious God in whom they can place their trust. He will not leave his people in the lurch. Luke writes to instill hope in his persecuted missionary communities. Through Luke-Acts he shows them how Jesus and they fit within the history of God's dealings with his people and thus offers them encouragement in their discussions with both Jews and Gentiles. But in asserting these last points, I am already on the threshold of Chapter 3 which deals with Luke's person and his situation. To that I now turn.

3
Luke the Author
and His Situation

Since most of my workshop and institute participants were keenly interested in knowing as much about Luke as soon as they could, I presume that my readers have the same interests. As you work through the remainder of this book, you will be able to detect the evidence which further substantiates the positions I assume here.

I. Luke the Author

We have no family album, no self-portrait of Luke. We must surmise from Luke-Acts about his person. At this juncture, I recall the question raised by one institute participant: "On the basis of your studies, what do you imagine Luke was like?" In what follows I answer that question by moving toward the center of the sphere of Luke the person from different positions.

A. *Luke Is Not a Physician*

My first image of Luke is a negative one. There is little evidence that Colossians 4:14 refers to our author: "Luke the beloved physician and Demas greet you." Despite passages like Luke 4:38, 5:12, and 8:44, the overwhelming conclusion to be drawn from the evidence of the language of Luke-Acts is that Luke was not a physician. Luke seems to use medical language the way we use Freudian terminology like "a Freudian slip." The Freudian terminology is in the air, part of our culture, and our use of it does not prove that we have ever read a word of Freud or are practicing psychoanalysts.

B. *Luke Is Not a Companion of Paul*

In the Acts of the Apostles there are four "we" passages: 16:10-17; 20:5-15; 21:1-18; 27:1—28:16. These passages are often cited as evidence that Luke, the author of Acts, traveled with Paul and was an eyewitness of the events narrated. But I am being more persuaded of the opinion that the "we" of these sections is the literary "we" which an author employs to enliven an account of sea journeys and does not mean that the author was onboard ship. This opinion helps me account for the fact that very soon after Paul and his companions disembark on land, the "we" style trails off.

To champion the author of Luke-Acts as a

companion of Paul, one must also solve the problem that the Paul whom Luke describes in Acts is often out of step with the Paul of the letters. Would a companion of Paul, who frequently insisted vigorously on his status as an apostle (see, e.g., 2 Corinthians 10—13), have failed to give the title of apostle to Paul? According to Luke's definition of an apostle, Paul could not be an apostle since he had not been a witness to the earthly life of Jesus. (See Acts 1:21-22. But also check Acts 14:4, 14 where the spherical thinker Luke calls Paul an apostle.)

C. Luke, Elderly Statesman and Overseer of His Missionary Communities

In Chapter 1 I used the analogy of Luke the elderly statesman within his communities. This image helps me explain Luke's use of various traditions in his composition of Luke-Acts. I expand this image to include the aspect of overseer. I imagine Luke as situated in the main missionary community of Antioch, a community which has sent out missionaries and formed satellite missionary communities. Luke is the overseer of this missionary activity and is in charge of the debriefing of the missionaries who return with stories of how various people have received the message of Jesus. Luke also oversees the incorporation of new traditions about Jesus and the early Church into the mainstream of his communities' life. Some of these new traditions may have been the prize possessions of

Christians who fled Jerusalem just before its destruction in A.D. 70 and entered Luke's communities.

It seems that one reason why Luke can deal as well as he does with diverse traditions lies in the fact that he is bi-cultural. He is like the son of missionary parents who can speak fluent Chinese and English and is at home in and sympathetic to both cultures. Luke is both Jewish and Graeco-Roman. He can write the elegant Greek of Luke 1:1-4 and the translation Greek of Luke 1:5 — 2:52.

D. Luke the First Hagiographer

As we have seen in Chapter 2, Luke writes biblical history. And while writing that history, he is the first hagiographer, that is, the first author of the lives of the saints. He does not detail events in the lives of Jesus, Peter, Stephen, Philip and Paul for the sake of satisfying our curiosity of knowing some facts about these famous people of our history. As a good biblical historian, Luke is all intent on edifying his communities by means of the lives of the saints.

Take Paul for one example. Luke is not senile and out of touch with his material when he repeats Paul's call three times in Acts: 9:1-19, 22:1-16, and 26:9-18. Luke spotlights Paul as a model. For those missionaries who find preaching to the Jews very difficult, Paul serves as an example of how God can surprise even the most staunch Pharisee and merciless persecutor of the Church with a call to follow

Jesus. For Christians despondent because of seemingly interminable persecution, Paul is a model of hope. He is rescued from persecution time after time. It is with hope gleaming in his eyes that Luke writes: "But Jews came there from Antioch and Iconium; and having persuaded the people, they stoned Paul and dragged him out of the city, supposing that he was dead. But when the disciples gathered about him, he rose up and entered the city; and on the next day he went on with Barnabas to Derbe" (Acts 14:19-20).

Luke invites his readers to recall their history, to meditate upon it, to see God at work in the lives of their forebears and heroes, and thus be enabled to see God's actions in their own lives and to move with confidence into the future to which God lures them.

E. Luke the Pastoral Theologian and Dreamer

Luke, the elderly statesman and overseer, is also a pastoral theologian. He is not a systematic theologian in the style of a Hans Küng, Karl Rahner, or Paul Tillich, each of whom integrates experience, theological traditions, and philosophy into some vast system. Luke is like the pastor who applies theology to meet various situations. He is like the sensitive pastor who, on the issue of divorce and remarriage, can lay out the various options with insight and compassion.

But Luke is, above all, a dreamer, a visionary

for his troubled Church, some of whose members are ready to throw in the towel. He is like a keynote speaker who lifts the drooping spirits of the assembly and fires them with hope. He is like the lecturer who is applauded on every side because his vision helps dispel the confusion of living in the post-Vatican II Roman Catholic Church. For those who almost despair of going the Christian Way alone, Luke projects the vision of the strength and support to be found in community (see Acts 2:41-47 and 4:31-35).

In answering the question of how I imagine Luke, I have flirted with a description of his situation. It is time to court that topic.

II. Luke's Situation

Luke's situation can be succinctly described as one in which the burning issue is the Jewish question. We explore that situation on three levels: persecution, search for continuity amid discontinuity, and mission to the Jews. The reader will easily spot the interrelationships of all three points.

A. Persecution

Luke's fifty-two chapters abound with so much material on rejection and persecution that it seems reasonable to assume that this was a major factor in his situation. But in order to appreciate the nature of the persecution which Luke's communities were experiencing, we will have to divest ourselves of our Hollywood mentality of seeing Christians thrown to the lions. The persecution most often encountered by Luke's communities was informal, in the nature of economic boycott and reprisal. Persecutors could cut off a family's lifeline by refusing to take in the sons as apprentices. Although the Christians may not have had to contend with the roaring lions, the persecution they experienced was sharp and long-lasting.

It seems that Jews were the chief persecutors. Acts 4:3, 5:18, 8:3, 12:4 and 22:19 refer to Jewish imprisonment of Christians. In 2 Corinthians 11:24 Paul gives independent evidence of Jewish persecution of Christians when he notes that five times he suffered the Jewish punishment of being flogged forty times less one (see Karris, "Missionary Communities").

The persecution factor in Luke-Acts helps us find an angle by which we can anticipate the difficult subject of Luke's theology of Jesus' death. Luke's predominant view of Jesus' death is that Jesus did not die on the cross to save us from our sins. In Luke-Acts Jesus dies as a martyr. Luke's depiction of Jesus' death as that of a martyr speaks eloquent volumes to his persecuted communities. It is a powerful theology which Luke formulates as he places words of forgiveness and trust on the lips of Jesus the martyr and on the lips of Stephen, the first Christian martyr. More detail on this vitally important point can be found in Chapter 5.

An appreciation of the persecution situation in which Luke and his communities find themselves opens the door to the meaning of Luke's preface (Luke 1:1-4). For communities which are suffering persecution and wondering whether the Lord is present, Luke writes biblical history which will assure them that their faith and hope are well founded. Their God is The Faithful God.

B. Search for Continuity amid Discontinuity

The point of a search for continuity amid discontinuity can seem obscure at best until we remember situations in which we have been blown loose from our life moorings. Recall how we felt at the death of a loved one. How were we going to make it without that person? How does a divorced person discover continuity in a life which has been shattered, upended, spilled out like a broken egg? How does a retired person cope with separation from friends at work, with a self-concept that equated one's usefulness with working from nine to five? How does one continue life when one has hit the ripe old age of thirty and is depressed because our culture cautions that senility is lurking around the next corner?

There is enough evidence in the Lukan themes of fulfillment of promise and rejection to suspect that Luke is very much concerned with the issue of how the Christian Way (Acts 9:2) builds upon what God has done for the Jewish people in the past. We can imagine Luke's communities being troubled by some Jewish synagogues in the area. Such harassment becomes more widespread around A.D. 85 when the Pharisees became the dominant voice in Judaism by consolidating their forces and silencing opposing voices. The Pharisees would lay claim to God's promises and refute from Scripture the claim that God has fulfilled his promises in Jesus and the Christian community. These arguments might easily paint Christians into the corner of doubting that they were heirs of God's promises.

Luke's biblical history explains the Christian Way. Jesus is indeed the fulfillment of God's promises. In appointing twelve apostles, Jesus went about the work of restoring Israel under the symbol of the primordial twelve patriarchs. These twelve, whose number was renewed with the election of Matthias (Acts 1:12-26), continue the work begun by the Messiah Jesus and preach to the Jews and to all nations. While the Jewish rulers reject Jesus, his apostles and Paul, other Jews are won over to the Christian Way. Through these converts (see Acts 2:41), there is continuity between the Israel of God's promises and the Christian Way. Because he is subject to the apostles in Jerusalem, Paul is the link of continuity between the Christians of Luke's day, the twelve apostles, and Jesus. Moreover, Paul, as a staunch Pharisee (see Acts 26:5) and a firm believer in God's promise of the resurrection (Acts 26:6-8), is a prime example of how continuous the Christian Way is with God's promises as recorded in the Scriptures.

Luke-Acts is written to encourage those who are beginning to doubt that their faith is well founded, who feel themselves cut loose on the sea of doubt because their bonds of continuity with the past are being severed.

C. Mission to the Jews

Against the tide of scholarly opinion, I contend that one of Luke's main concerns is to inspire his communities to continue their mission to the Jews. Paul's quotation of the strong words of Isaiah in Acts 28:26-27 should not be used as proof positive that Luke's communities have shut the door on the Jews. Acts 28:26-28 repeats a refrain which is also instanced in Acts 18:6-7: "And when they (the Jews of Corinth) opposed and reviled Paul, he shook out his garments and said to them, 'Your blood be upon your heads! I am innocent. From now on I will go to the Gentiles.' " Paul's strong gesture and words do not prevent him from continuing his preaching to the Jews in Ephesus, the next city he approaches on mission. As in Acts 28:24, some Jews believe whereas others are stubborn (compare Acts 19:8-9). Luke uses Paul, his communities' bond of continuity with the twelve apostles and Jesus, as the exemplary missionary, who despite all opposition continues his preaching to the Jews. Death prevented Paul from preaching beyond Rome. Luke's communities must follow in Paul's footsteps and continue his preaching both in intensity and breadth. This is the way Luke-Acts hangs from its ending and inspires days of meditation in its readers (see Chapter 2).

In sum, Luke and his communities are agitated by the Jewish question. While showing his communities how they stand in continuity with God's fulfillment of his promises, with Jesus, with the twelve apostles, and with Paul, Luke is also concerned to build them up in their identity as followers of Jesus. He accomplishes this latter task to a large extent through the travel narrative of Luke 9:51—19:44, which contains material on mission (10:1-24) and unique materials on the cost and joys of discipleship. But he forms his readers primarily by the picture he paints of God. It is to this picture of The Faithful God that we now turn.

4
The Faithful God

In this chapter I will examine the cardinal point of Luke's theology. Some of the material discussed earlier will come into clearer focus as we view two sides of the same coin: God-faithful-to-promises; the God of Surprises.

I. God-Faithful-to-Promises

In this section I will first share images and examples to aid us in our thinking of The Faithful God, then I will explore Luke 7:18-35, and finally I will offer my lived view of Luke's theology of The Faithful God.

A. Images and Examples

When the weatherman predicts a spectacularly fine weekend, and it's cold, dreary, and rainy, we say that he was mistaken. When a person breaks a promise, we say that he or she is untrustworthy or was perhaps powerless to keep the promise.

The boy in the movie "A Hero Ain't Nothing But A Sandwich" refuses to trust the promises which his new father makes to him. His first father deserted him. The boy does not want to be heartbroken again, so he puts a huge padlock around his heart.

A student of mine has made a helpful distinction between the literal form of a promise and the essential form of a promise. She uses the example of her mother and father promising to one another that if either of them got sick the other would not confine the sick party to a nursing home. As events turned out, her mother had to break the literal form of the promise by putting her husband into a nursing home. In doing so she preserved the essential form, namely, love and care for her spouse.

I conclude with a homey example: These past months my mother, a very lovely and active lady, has taken to making clowns to cheer people up. Using a dishwater detergent bottle for the body, she customizes clown clothes and faces for the individual recipient. Recently I asked her for a bright clown and had some idea in the back of my mind of the bright clown I expected. Mom surprised me with a professor clown, with hand-tailored black suit, Roman collar, and two black hats to cover his bald head. That clown did not fit my expectation of a bright clown. Mom remarked that the professor was me years from now and that professors by definition are bright. Two hours after being gifted with my bright clown, my disappointment turned to joy and laughter. My mother had surprised me with a most elegantly dressed bright clown, and my expectation of what she should have given me almost blinded me to that surprise and closed my heart to the joy of fulfillment. She had kept the essential form of her promise to make me a bright clown.

In the two parts which follow I will have occasion to refer back to these images and examples. They are important because they are the means by which I invite you to think Luke's thoughts and mine about The Faithful God.

B. *Example of Luke 7:18-35*

From this long and signal passage we single out two points for comment. First, through two of his disciples John the Baptist asks Jesus, "Are you he who is to come, or shall we look for another?" (7:19). "He who is to come" is the name of a person who was to come to accomplish God's will. From Luke 3:15-17 it seems that John the Baptist expected a fire-and-brimstone fulfillment of the promise of "he who is to come." After performing miracles in the presence of John's two witnesses, Jesus sends them back with: "Go and tell John what you have seen and heard: the blind receive their sight, the lame walk, lepers are cleansed, and the deaf hear, the dead are raised up, the poor have good news preached to them. And blessed is he who takes no offense at me" (7:22-23). The narration of what Jesus did is based on passages from the prophet Isaiah (29:18-19; 35:5-6; 61:1) and harkens back to the description of Jesus' ministry found in Luke 4:18-19. What Jesus does is in fulfillment of God's promises. In the person of John the Baptist Luke asks his readers: "Are you going to be scandalized because Jesus doesn't meet your expectations?" Whatever pre-conceived notions of the "Messiah" people may have entertained, Luke directs them to go back to the drawing board because of the actual facts of Jesus' life, death, resurrection, and sending of the Spirit.

The second point of this example is couched in Luke 7:29-30: "When they heard this, all the people and the tax collectors justified God, having been baptized with the baptism of John; but the Pharisees and the lawyers rejected the purpose of God for themselves, not having been baptized by him." The leaders of the Jewish people—the ones who would have been expected to accept John's preaching—reject God's purpose, his fulfillment of his promise of forgiveness and life. The least likely candidates for the position of accepting God's offer of forgiveness say a big Yes to that offer.

To conclude and anticipate at the same time, people who hold God to one promise and cling to their literal interpretation of that promise find it difficult to see the God of Surprises at work in their lives. John the Baptist, the Pharisees and lawyers present challenges to all to see whether their convictions are born of rigidity rather than of faith.

C. My Lived View of
Luke's Theology of The Faithful God

In this section I make a down-payment of my view of Luke's theology of The Faithful God. Further installments will be paid below in the section on the God of Surprises and in Chapters 5, 6 and 7.

It takes time for fulfillment of promises to occur. Simeon and Anna do not seem atypical in this regard (Luke 2:25-35). Our culture may instill in us a desire for instantaneous answers and fulfillments of promises, but like a lifetime of faithful married life, it takes time for promises to be fulfilled. I think there is more delight in experiencing The Faithful God in the process of fulfilling his promises of life and wholeness than in experiencing the actual fulfillment.

One author is on to something profound when he observes: "Each promise in the history of Israel is definitely though partially fulfilled, and each such fulfillment gives way to a new promise" (Paul S. Minear, *To Heal and To Reveal*. N.Y., 1976, p. 85). After being forced by Jesus' resurrection to alter their views of him, the disciples appreciate how he is the fulfillment of God's promises (see Luke 24:13-35). But that fulfillment opens up to another promise, namely, that forgiveness of sins in his name must be preached to all nations. Because the disciples have experienced God's fidelity in this one regard, they have deeper trust that he will fulfill his new promise. The fulfillment of God's call to me to religious life and priesthood has opened up new promises whose process of fulfillment I enjoy more and more with each passing year.

To me Luke has developed an entire theology of The Faithful God who fulfills his promises. He tries to detect God's action in the present and his direction for the future by searching how he has acted in the past. If a pattern can be found in God's previous actions, there is insight into the present and hope for the future. That's why Luke interprets so much of the Christian Way by means of Scripture in the speeches of Acts. He wants his readers to put on his mentality. His construction of Stephen's speech in Acts 7 is a good example of how he probes the present on the basis of the past.

In my own life, I have begun to realize more fully that I must claim more and more of the Judaeo-Christian tradition as my past, so that I have a broader basis for seeing God's action in my life. My Western culture has made me too individualistic as if everything revolves around me and my importance. While I may be unique, I can learn immeasurably about The Faithful God from the ways he has acted in the lives of others. And as I assume more and more of the Judaeo-Christian tradition as my roots, I will be able to see God's handwriting more clearly. I now personally know that God disciplines those he loves. That is not just a truth from the Judaeo-Christian tradition. I am also resolving to let the Spirit interpret my past joyfully, heal my memories of hurt and injuries, and direct me into the future.

I am thankful for the God who has been operative in my past, even though it may have taken me some time to decipher his handwriting. Because I have experienced The Faithful God in a moment of darkness, I trust that he will be with me at other dark times. I have stripped the huge padlock off my heart and sold it for scrap metal.

II. The God of Surprises

In this section, as in section I, we begin by offering images and examples; then we provide examples from Luke-Acts, and finally discuss training to be open to the God of Surprises.

A. Images and Examples

While many of the images and examples from the section on The Faithful God can be transferred to this consideration of the other side of the same coin, we still need to prime the pump somewhat. There is the surprise birthday party, the surprise baby shower. I have been surprised by the grandeur of a golf course during the blossoming of spring— and by my good golf score! It's the surprise we experience when a person shares life with us. It's the surprise of a bright professor clown!

Centuries ago the philosopher Heraclitus taught: "Unless you expect the unexpected, you will never find truth, for it is hard to discover and hard to attain." We are not only surprised by the unexpected, but unless we expect the unexpected we will not find truth.

B. Examples from Luke-Acts

Luke's parables are his best examples of the God of Surprises. Billions of readers have delighted in the God of Surprises portrayed in the Parable of the Prodigal Son (Luke 15:11-32). For the young boy who thinks that he is no longer worthy to be called son, the compassionate and loving father surprises him and throws a party. Most of us relish the Parable of the Publican and the Pharisee (Luke 18:9-14) until we learn that the publican was a toll collector who was considered a traitor to his country and was labeled an outcast. The Pharisee was a paragon of virtue. The parable surprises us, in that the outcast is welcomed whereas the person who was busily counting up his merits is rejected. It takes most of us a long time to get over the shock that the God of Surprises offers salvation unconditionally, that we cannot buy it.

Acts 8:1-4 contains two theological messages. The first one is that the apostles remain in Jerusalem as symbols of the bond of continuity with Israel while a full-scale persecution rages around them and scatters every other Christian. The second truth is the surprise that growth is the outcome of suffering. For those who know from experience that suffering leads to growth, this truth makes great sense and may not be a surprise. But for those members of Luke's communities who were suffering persecution, this surprising truth gives light, support, and hope.

In Acts 10:19, 44, 47 and 11:12, 15, Luke underscores the fact that Peter would never have engaged in missionary work to the Gentile Cornelius if he had not been surprised by the Holy Spirit. As we will see in Chapter 8, the Spirit is God's agent of surprise. Bearers of the promise, like Peter, are not in control of the fulfillment of promise.

Further instances could be given of the God of Surprises at work in Luke-Acts. But sufficient have been provided, I hope, to give you a glimpse of the God whose story is told in the lives of the actors of Luke-Acts.

C. Training To Be Open
   to the God of Surprises

There are no five easy lessons on how to be open to the God of Surprises. Let me circle this truth. Following in the footsteps of Francis of Assisi who was surprised by God in his ministry to the lepers, I have learned that God has surprised me in the person of the "outcasts" I have invited into my life. I am doing my best to give the God of Surprises room to operate in. I must risk wandering into the land of surprises and away from my turf where I have installed a sophisticated alarm system to alert me to God's presence. Life, and not rigor mortis, should begin at forty for yours truly. It would be sheer joy to develop the attitude of open-handedness which permitted Mary to be surprised by Gabriel's message. In Chapters 6, 7 and 8 I will return to this meditation on how to be ready for the advent of the God of Surprises.

5
Jesus and
The Faithful God

I will treat some of Luke's richest themes in this chapter: table fellowship and the breaking of bread; Jesus dies as the model of hope; Jesus' saving significance.

I. Table Fellowship and the Breaking of Bread

A jokester once remarked that in Luke's Gospel Jesus is always eating. There is a considerable amount of truth in this observation, for there is nary a chapter in Luke's Gospel which does not contain a reference to eating. Since I cannot cover all these passages, I will limit myself to some remarks about table fellowship, the breaking of bread, and Luke's situation.

A. Table Fellowship

Let me ask you some questions. Do you like to eat alone? Do you like to eat with someone you don't like? Do you celebrate Christmas and Easter with family and friends? How do you feel when you do not receive an invitation to a party you really want to attend? Does your image of heaven contain the element of a banquet with those you love?

Our abbreviated game of twenty questions is meant to get us into imagining readiness to understand Luke's theme of table fellowship. Jesus' table fellowship, as underlined by Luke, is best explained from an Old Testament background. God offers communion to his people by inviting them to a banquet: "On this mountain, Yahweh Sabaoth will prepare for all peoples a banquet of rich food, a banquet of fine wines, of food rich and juicy, of fine strained wines" (Jerusalem Bible translation).

Luke's Jesus is revolutinary as he acts out the meaning of the kingdom he preaches by eating with outcasts, sinners, and toll collectors. Jesus cracks wide open the prized image of table fellowship which limited God's table companions to the righteous. By his actions Jesus reveals a God who welcomes and makes merry with those who fall outside the pale of society's good will. By associating and joyfully banqueting with sinners, Jesus challenges the way his society withholds the promise of life and forgiveness from some of its citizenry. Jesus is a window to God who offers communion to all people—outcasts, sinners, and women too.

I refer to the following passages as evidence for the points I have just made:

And Levi made him a great feast in his house;

and there was a large company of tax collectors
and others sitting at table with them. And the
Pharisees and their scribes murmured against
his disciples saying, "Why do you eat and
drink with tax collectors and sinners?" (Luke
5:29-30).

Now the tax collectors and sinners were all
drawing near to hear him. And the Pharisees
and the scribes murmured, saying, "This man
receives sinners and eats with them" (Luke
15:1-2).

And when they saw it they all murmured, "He
has gone in to be the guest of a man who is a
sinner" (Luke 19:7).

So when Peter went up to Jerusalem, the cir-
cumcision party criticized him, saying, "Why
did you go to uncircumcised men and eat with
them?" (Acts 11:2-3).

The murmurers and the critics in these four
passages know who should be invited to table fellowship and who should not. They hold the reins of
the invitation list in their hands. Small wonder that
they are not open to the God of Surprises, revealed
by Jesus, a God who in his compassion delights in
inviting the unexpected.

Speaking of unexpected guests at banquet reminds me of Luke 14:12-14: "He said also to the
man who had invited him, 'When you give a dinner

or a banquet, do not invite your friends or your brothers or your kinsmen or rich neighbors, lest they also invite you in return, and you be repaid. But when you give a feast, invite the poor, the maimed, the lame, the blind, and you will be blessed, because they cannot repay you. You will be repaid at the resurrection of the just.' " The parable of the banquet which follows immediately repeats the listing of those to be invited: "the poor and maimed and blind and lame" (14:21). The poor are joined to those who would be excluded from Jewish worship. All of them are guests of honor. In Jesus, God's merciful heart excludes no one and embraces all.

At the Last Supper Jesus surprises his disputing disciples: "Let the greatest among you become as the youngest, and the leader as one who serves. For which is the greater, one who sits at table, or one who serves? Is it not the one who sits at table? But *I am among you as one who serves*" (Luke 22:26-27). Table fellowship in the Christian community must be defined by who Jesus is. Power-grabbing must give way to love of others. But in discussing this aspect of table fellowship, I am beginning to move across the borders of one symbol into that of another, the breaking of bread.

B. *The Breaking of Bread*

The risen Lord Jesus is recognized in the

Scriptures and in the Eucharist/breaking of bread:
"When he was at table with them, he took bread,
and blessed and broke it, and gave it to them. And
their eyes were opened and they recognized him;
and he vanished out of their sight. . . . Then they
told what had happened on the road, and how he
was known to them in the breaking of the bread"
(Luke 24:30-31, 35). As Luke shows in the key
summary passage of Acts 2:42, 46, the breaking of
bread is an essential part of what it means to be
community.

There are two additional passages in Acts
where breaking of bread is mentioned. While the
data is not crystal-clear, it seems that Luke is using
his communities' experiences of the effects of the
Eucharist/breaking of bread to interpret a miracle
story (Acts 20:7-12) and Paul's safety during a vi-
olent storm at sea (Acts 27:35). As Joachim Wanke
observes, later Christian communities can imitate
the community at Troas and be encouraged and
comforted because at the breaking of bread the
same Lord is present who at Troas saved the boy
through Paul. In Acts 27:35 Luke reminds his communities that when the breaking of bread is celebrated, salvation occurs (see 27:20, 31, 34) and help
is present in the most extreme circumstances. (See
Wanke, *Beobachtungen zum Eucharistiever-
ständnis des Lukas auf Grund der lukanischen
Mahlberichte*. Leipzig, 1973.)

At this point I cannot avoid saying a word or
two about the vexed question of whether Luke

22:19b-20 is original or was added by a later copyist:
" ' . . . which is given for you. Do this in remembrance of me.' And likewise the cup after supper,
saying, 'This cup which is poured out for you is the
new covenant in my blood.' " If the passage I have
just cited is not original, then the Eucharistic cele-
brations in Luke's communities did not contain a
reference to Jesus' death as vicarious suffering for
sins (see the words "given for you" and "poured out
for you"). Aware of the pitfalls of trying to make
Luke a linear thinker, I opt for the view that Luke
22:19b-20 is original and that Luke does know of a
tradition in which Jesus' death and consequently
the Eucharist is for sins. But Luke also knows another tradition and perhaps is more at home with it
because of his persecution and despair-prone situation. That tradition views the Eucharist/breaking of
bread as a continuation of Jesus' ministry of table
fellowship. Just as Jesus' table fellowship with outcasts and sinners was a joyful anticipatory celebra-
tion of the heavenly banquet, so too the Church in
its breaking of bread enjoys now—in anticipation—the joys of the messianic, heavenly feast. The
nature of the anticipation and the heavenly feast
itself are now determined by the life of Jesus. Put in
terms of the theology of The Faithful God, Jesus is
present at the breaking of bread primarily as the
risen Lord who trusted that God would be faithful to
his promises and not as one who died in our stead.
More detail on these aspects of Luke's view of how
Jesus saves will be forthcoming in sections II and
III below.

C. Luke's Situation

Like their Lord Jesus, Luke's communities are criticized for their association with outcasts. Their Jewish opponents give them the third degree for receiving unclean and unholy people into their ranks. Luke's persecuted communities are assured by the presence of the risen Lord at the breaking of bread that God is faithful to his promises and that the Lord is not an absentee landlord. In the examples of the boy at Troas and Paul on the high seas, the Lord has shown how he is present to save. But at times that saving presence can only be seen in retrospect, after one has been through the ordeal. With that sobering truth in mind, we turn to Luke's presentation of Jesus, the friend of outcasts, who died an outcast.

II. Luke 23:32-49:
Jesus' Death on the Cross

Before entering into a detailed discussion of this passage, I want to invite you to walk down a path with me. In exploring the meaning of Luke-Acts, I have recently been heavily influenced by the thought of the philosopher Gabriel Marcel (e.g., *Creative Fidelity*. N.Y., 1964) and his interpreter K. T. Gallagher (*The Philosophy of Gabriel Marcel*. N.Y., 1962). Under their tutelage I have gained insight into the meaning of Jesus' death. Here's the path they have laid out for us.

Our fidelity creates us. In being faithful to the person to whom we have committed ourselves, we bind up our futures and create ourselves. Our future is not like some movie reels which are played through our minds. By our fidelity we create the future. Lest this seem very dense, allow me to use my own life as an example. Some thirteen years ago I committed myself to a God who was calling me to teach Scripture. And in my year-in-and-year-out quest to be faithful to that God I have created myself and continue to do so. As I sit at this typewriter today composing my fifth book so that God's word might be better understood and lived, I recall the embarrassment of the Harvard summer school of 1966 when I, a theology major, strained to learn Greek with classics majors. I came close to shutting down the newly opened shop of my Scripture vocation. My future was surely not a series of movie reels running through my mind. Nor was yours. Through your pledge of fidelity, for example, to your spouse or to a dear friend, you created and continue to create yourself.

These reflections on creative fidelity help me to appreciate Jesus' death on the cross. To the end he is faithful to the compassionate God whom he proclaimed in word and in table fellowship. His fidelity to God created him as the fearless prophet who befriends the scum of society. While recognizing that these reflections may seem to go contrary to what Luke has to say in his infancy narrative about Jesus, the Son of God, I am content to develop this aspect of Luke's spherical thought.

In Luke's Gospel Jesus goes to his death as a prophet-martyr. In his meditations on the meaning of life, Marcel opens up another lush path for our reflections on Jesus' death. Ask yourself what your life is. Is it your works, what you have accomplished with your life? Partially, but not fully, because you are still living your life. Might it not be that what is essential to your life and mine is that which transcends our lives and gives justification for them? In answer to this question, Marcel uses the example of the martyr. His words deserve quotation in full:

> On the other hand, the person who is carrying the act out has, without any doubt at all, the feeling that through self-sacrifice he is reaching self-fulfillment; given his own situation and that of everything dear to him, he realizes his own nature most completely, he most completely *is*, in the act of giving his life away. . . . It is only from this point of view, that is to say, in a way that we can only express in a rather negative fashion, that it is possible to conceive how it could be that what we call the death of these men might also have been the summit, the culmination peak, of what we call their lives (*The Mystery of Being* I. Chicago, 1960, pp. 205-206).

Traveling along the path of these reflections, we now proceed to a consideration of Luke 23:32-49.

Luke 23:32-33: Jesus is crucified. We are so familiar with the sight of a crucified Jesus hanging on a cross that it may be hard for us to rethink ourselves into what really happened to Jesus. He was subjected to the most cruel punishment the Romans knew. Think of some punishments closer to home like being hanged, drawn and quartered, or being napalmed to death. Think past our American funeral practices which make a person who has suffered immensely "look so beautiful," as the sympathy-wishers put it. The Jesus who "came to seek and to save the lost" (Luke 19:10) is found among outcasts and criminals.

Luke 23:34: While suffering as an innocent prophet and martyr (see 23:4, 14-15, 22, 47, 51 on the theme of Jesus' innocence), Jesus continues his mission of offering forgiveness. It is of primal significance for Luke's persecuted communities that Jesus and Stephen, the first Christian martyr (Acts 7:60), forgive those who do them wrong.

Luke 23:35: As we have had occasion to mention earlier in Chapter 2, Luke separates the people from the Jewish leaders.

Luke 23:42-43: True to his mission of wrapping the arms of God's mercy around the outcasts, Jesus culminates his ministry and offers life to the "good thief." Today the thief will be with Jesus in paradise.

Luke 23:46: "Then Jesus, crying with a loud voice, said, 'Father, into thy hands I commit my spirit!' And having said this he breathed his last." For me this is the key verse of Luke-Acts. Jesus, condemned by the Jewish authorities who represented God to his people, and crucified by the civil authorities, is bereft of support in this life. Jesus, who had begun a trust walk with his God, whom he called Father, is faithful to that God to the end. With darkness all about him, perhaps the darkness of evil (see Luke 1:79 and 22:53), Jesus hands himself over to the Father. Hoping against hope, he gives himself completely to the Father and sums up his life in one word. Jesus fully creates himself by giving himself away into the hands of a trustworthy Father. Jesus, who had spent his entire ministry doing good, dies an outcast.

In its search for continuity amid discontinuity and in its suffering of persecution, Luke directs his communities' gaze toward Jesus hanging on the cross. When it seemed that the lights were going out, when no one cared, when there was not a glimmer of hope, Jesus trusted in God, his Father. The God, whose mercy and compassion Jesus had proclaimed by sharing table fellowship with outcasts, did not abandon Jesus. The Faithful Father raised him from the dead.

These past two years I have often meditated on Luke 23:32-49. I have shared some of the fruit of that meditation on the preceding pages. If asked to give a thumbnail sketch of my meditations, I would say, "Life is not cruel, unfair. God is gracious."

III. How Does Jesus Save?

Although New Testament writers commonly

interpret Jesus' death as a death in atonement for sins, that is not the only New Testament view of Jesus' death. John, for example, maintains that Jesus saves us by revealing to us the knowledge that God loves us (See J. T. Forestell, *The Word of the Cross*. Rome, 1974). Luke has his own way of showing how Jesus saves. The conservative evangelical scholar I. Howard Marshall concedes: "The atoning significance of the death of Jesus is not altogether absent from Acts, but it is not the aspect which Luke has chosen to stress. His presentation of the saving work of Jesus is consequently one-sided. . . . What is lacking is rather a full understanding of the significance of the cross as the means of salvation" (*Luke: Historian and Theologian*. Grand Rapids, 1971, p. 175). Although Marshall may be contrasting Luke unfavorably with Paul, he is correct in asserting that Luke does not highlight Jesus' death as atonement for sins. But why does Luke develop this position?

I suggest that there are two reasons why Luke doesn't accentuate the atoning significance of Jesus' death. The first reason stems from the fact that Luke writes biblical history (see Chapter 2). From the perspective of biblical history, in which God is the central actor, it is difficult for Luke to argue to the saving significance of Jesus, who is one prophet among many of God's will. Luke is spherical as he has Peter *affirm* the saving significance of Jesus rather than argue for it: "And there is salvation in no one else, for there is no other name under heaven given among men by which we must be saved"

(Acts 4:12). Luke the spherical thinker depicts the prophet Jesus proclaiming that a merciful Father offers forgiveness to sinners who repent, e.g., in the Parable of the Prodigal Son. But Jesus himself does not mediate this forgiveness. At the same time Luke does talk about Jesus as the one who mediates forgiveness of sins to those who believe in him (Acts 2:38).

To summarize this first point, since Luke has adopted the framework of biblical history, he has difficulty attributing saving significance to Jesus and his death. There is indeed salvation in Jesus' name, but Luke cannot substantiate this claim from his vantage point of salvation history. But this vantage point does help Luke make other key statements about the meaning of Jesus. The martyrdom of the prophet Jesus points to the validity of his teaching of God's will since he was willing to die rather than abandon God's revelation. Luke's portrayal of Jesus as a prophet provides a common ground for his communities' dialogues with potential Jewish converts since prophet is a familiar Jewish and biblical category. Luke's description of the hope-filled martyr Jesus going to death inspires Luke's communities as they face persecution and the prospect of martyrdom. In Luke-Acts the men of the Spirit (see Chapter 8) continue what Jesus proclaimed but now proclaim it in his name and by his authority. (In developing this first point I am under heavy debt to the 1975 University of Chicago dissertation by Waldemar Schmeichel, "Soteriology in the Theology of Luke.")

The second reason why Luke downplays the atoning significance of Jesus' death is anchored in his view that Jesus' death is the culmination of his revelation of God as a trustworthy Father. This revelation effects salvation. Jesus' death on the cross in complete trust in his gracious Father points to what salvation means. Jesus' revelation of the Father, especially on the cross, provides release from all the gods in which we humans place our trust — money, personal virtue, power. Jesus trusts his Father and reveals that the salvation of humankind is to be found in such trusting and not in grasping at things which are no-gods. Jesus' offering of himself in complete trust to a loving Father blazes a trail to what it means to be fully human. Jesus, the person of hope, garners all the strands of his life and in complete trust commits his spirit to his Father. To Jesus' expression of complete fidelity and trust the Father answers in the resurrection and the power of the Spirit at Pentecost. (See L. E. Keck, *A Future for the Historical Jesus*. Nashville, 1971, pp. 185, 234; G. Voss, *Die Christologie der lukanischen Schriften in Grundzügen*. Paris, 1965, p. 130.)

For Luke's communities who suffer persecution because of their faith in Jesus, who are tempted to despair of the Lord's care, who are tempted to find security in possessions, Jesus' trust in his Father shows where salvation lies.

In conclusion, I paraphrase Gabriel Marcel and say that meditating on Jesus-faithful-to-his-Father-till-death exorcises despair. I have found such meditation a powerful antidote to the sickness of despair which tried to make inroads in me after the death of my sister.

6
Prayer: Access to The Faithful God

On our journey through this chapter we follow three roads: the Lukan passages on petitionary prayer, key Lukan prayer passages, and the inter-relatedness of Lukan themes.

*   *   *

I. Petitionary Prayer in Luke-Acts

If I merely tell you that prayer is an important theme in Luke-Acts, you could well put on a Missouri attitude and bark: "Show me!" So show you, I will. After listing representative passages in which Luke alone mentions prayer, I will probe the reasons why Luke stresses petitionary prayer. In this section I make liberal use of P. T. O'Brien, "Prayer in Luke-Acts," *Tyndale Bulletin* 24 (1973), pp. 111-127.

A. Gospel of Luke

(1) Examples of People Praying

1:13—Zechariah's prayer for a son has been heard.

3:21—The Spirit is given to Jesus in answer to prayer; see also Luke 11:13; Acts 1:14; 2:1-4; 4:23-31; 8:15-17.

5:16—Jesus withdraws alone to pray.

6:12—Jesus prays before he chooses the twelve apostles.

9:18—Jesus prays before Peter makes his confession that Jesus is "the Christ of God."

9:28-29—Jesus is transfigured as he prays.

22:32—Jesus prays for Simon Peter that his faith not fail.

22:39-46—Twofold admonition, "Pray that you may not enter into temptation" on the Mount of Olives.

23:34—"Father, forgive them; for they know not what they do."

23:46—"Father, into thy hands I commit my spirit!"

(2) Teaching on Prayer

(a) Lukan Parables

11:5-8—Persistence in prayer.

18:1-8—Don't lose heart; continue to pray during persecution even though the Lord seems to delay.

18:9-14—The person praying should have a true
        dependence on God.

*(b) Luke 11:13 in Contrast to Matthew 7:11 —gift of
    the Holy Spirit (see below for more detail).*

B. The Acts of the Apostles

(1) Similarities with the Gospel

In Chapter 2 I pointed out some passages which
showed Luke's literary and theological skill in join-
ing his Gospel and Acts. Here are some passages
which add further support to that observation. The
early Christian community follows the example of
Jesus at prayer:

Acts 1:14—All devote themselves to prayer while
        waiting for the promised Holy Spirit. Recall
        Jesus at prayer in Luke 3:21.

Acts 1:24—The assembled 120 pray to know which
        person to select to replace the apostle Judas.
        See Jesus' prayer in Luke 6:12.

Acts 7:59—In imitation of Jesus, Stephen commits
        his spirit to the one in whom he has placed all
        his trust. See Luke 23:46.

Acts 7:60—In imitation of Jesus, Stephen prays,
        "Lord, do not hold this sin against them."
        See Luke 23:34.

Additional examples of Luke's portrayal of the early

Christian communities' imitation of Jesus at prayer can be found in Acts 2:41, 42, 47; 3:1; 12:5, 12; 16:25.

(2) *Prayer and the Mission of the Church*

Acts 1:24—Once the sacred number of twelve apostles is completed, the promised Spirit will come to impel the community to mission.

Acts 10:2, 4, 31—Cornelius' prayer is heard by the God of Surprises who sends Peter to the first Gentile convert.

Acts 13:1-3—The Spirit selects Paul and Barnabas for mission.

What an array of passages! Perhaps I overdid my response to "Show me!" In any case, let's try to make some sense of this mass of material. There are two paths open to us. The first is to evaluate the parallelism between the Gospel and Acts. A preliminary evaluation of these parallelisms shows that Luke directs his communities to pray in imitation of the early Christian communities which, in their turn, imitated Jesus at prayer. The second path is more tortuous. Luke's reasons for stressing prayer can best be discerned in those prayer passages in which he gives the content of the prayer, in which his modifications of tradition are clear, and in which

other key Lukan themes surface. In the next sections we pursue this second path.

II. *Key Prayer Passages in Luke-Acts*

In this section I will first discuss Luke 1:46-55
and Acts 4:24-31. Then I will turn my attention to
Luke 11:1-13 and 22:39-46. In treating the first set of
passages, I will underline the content of the prayers.
In investigating the second set of passages, I will
highlight Luke's modification of tradition. In both
discussions I will note other key Lukan themes. I
have developed many of my ideas for this section
from the masterful work of L. Monloubou, *La
prière selon saint Luc*. Paris, 1976.

A. *Luke 1:46-55 and Acts 4:24-31 —*
Detecting the Father's Hand

(1) Luke 1:46-55

This hymn of praise, Mary's Magnificat, opens
a door to Luke's vision of how his communities
should use God's prior fulfillment of his promises as
a basis for detecting his hand in the present. In
verses 46-49 Mary sings the praises of the God who
has graced her. In verse 50 she begins to interpret
what has happened to her by recalling how God has
acted in the past: "And his mercy is on those who
fear him from generation to generation." She con-

cludes this interpretation of her singular blessing with: "He has helped his servant Israel, in remembrance of his mercy, as he spoke to our fathers, to Abraham and to his posterity for ever" (1:54-55). Luke uses Mary's prayer to show that what God has done for her has not been done in isolation from his actions in the past. Mary interprets her present on the basis of the past of God's promises.

(2) Acts 4:24-31

In this passage Luke gives a mini-course on how to decipher the Lord's handwriting. The community interprets the persecution of the apostles by recalling and pondering what has happened to God's people and to Jesus in the past. Verse 24 recalls the prayer of King Hezekiah as he sought guidance from the Lord during Sennacherib's threat to Jerusalem's existence. That prayer begins in Isaiah 37:16 with: "O Lord of hosts, God of Israel, who art enthroned above the cherubim, thou art the God, thou alone, of all the kingdoms of the earth; thou hast made heaven and earth." Verses 25-26 feed in thoughts from Psalm 2:1-2. Verses 27-28 refer to the experience of Jesus, the persecuted person par excellence, and to God's providential care. Verses 29-30 apply these past dealings of God with his people to the present as the community prays for boldness. Their prayer is answered as verse 31 details. This model prayer interprets present experience on the basis of God's past dealings with his people and prays for strength for the present, so that the community can continue God's work in the future.

It seems obvious to me that what Luke describes in so few verses in Luke 1:46-55 and Acts 4:24-31 was the result of long soul-searching to detect the Father's hand. These passages give us a good glimpse of how Luke wants his communities to fashion their prayers. Confident that their God has been faithful in the past, they detect and interpret his action in the present.

B. Luke 11:1-13 and 22:39-46 —
 Seeking The Faithful God During Trial

(1) Luke 11:1-13

From this singularly rich passage which Luke has composed from traditional materials, we select a few items. To the disciples' request that Jesus teach them how to pray, he responds that they should address God as Father. "Father" recalls Jesus' prayer in Luke 10:21-22 and is a road sign directing us ahead to the summit of Luke 23:46: "Father, into thy hands I commit my spirit." For Jesus and his disciples God is Father with all that that symbol conveys. Jesus' disciples are to ask, seek, and knock. It is not always limpidly clear that God has fulfilled his promises or is in the process of being faithful by fulfilling them. One must ask, seek, and knock to spot God at work.

In 11:13 Luke concludes Jesus' teaching on prayer with: "If you then, who are evil, know how to give good gifts to your children, how much more will the heavenly Father give *the Holy Spirit* to those who ask him." In a similar passage Matthew has: "If you then, who are evil, know how to give good gifts to your children, how much more will your Father who is in heaven give *good things* to those who ask him" (7:11). Luke modifies common tradition with the words "the Holy Spirit" and invites us to reflect upon the stellar importance of the Holy Spirit in Luke-Acts (see Chapter 8). By means of this modification he directs our gaze to the theme of poor and rich (see Chapter 7). For the well-heeled members of Luke's communities, who may face loss of possessions because of persecution, it is more important to be promised the Holy Spirit as an answer to prayer than more worldly goods.

(2) Luke 22:39-46

A careful comparison of Luke 22:39-46 with its source, Mark 14:32-43, will show how Luke has streamlined his account of Jesus' prayer on the Mount of Olives. Gone is mention of Jesus making his rounds to check up on his sleeping disciples. Luke drops Mark's reference to Jesus praying three times. Luke puts Jesus' admonition to his disciples front and center stage by using it to bracket the entire scene: "Pray that you may not enter into temptation" (22:40, 46). Luke's advice to his communities, which continue in the trials of Jesus (see Luke 22:28), is that they, like Jesus, strengthen themselves through prayer lest temptation seize them. For Luke temptation is not to some sexual sin or aberration. It is the temptation to despair, to say good-bye to Jesus when all is black and God seems absent.

In sum, Luke urges his communities to pray not only because Jesus and the early Christian communities prayed. They should also pray to gain access to the will of The Faithful God. They should pray to gain guidance from the past for the present. Confident that their God will not abandon them, they should pray for strength to withstand the temptation to despair.

III. Interrelatedness of Lukan Themes

I conclude our exploration of Luke's reasons for emphasizing prayer by briefly showing how he relates the theme of prayer to his other key themes.

Prayer is very important for Luke and his communities as they labor to see continuity amid discontinuity, as they struggle to discern God's will while despair pounds at their door. The will of The Faithful God cannot be read straight-off as one might read off a newspaper headline. The prayer of seeking, asking, and knocking is necessary.

These are the models Luke presents to his communities—Jesus at prayer to his Father, the crucified Jesus who trusted that his God was faithful, the early Christian communities which sought God's will in the present by pondering his actions in the past. These are fine models for us, too. In prayer we seek to know and love the Father as trustworthy, we search for patterns in his past dealings with his people. Among people who say that the world is cruel and unjust, we strive to hold onto a gracious God. We strive to utter Father, a word which beckons us to see God through Jesus' eyes—a word which suggests a gracious presence, the depths of a person, the mystery of a love experienced. Let's pray as Jesus did: "Father God."

7
Poor and Rich

During supper at a recent institute some of the participants told me that they were eagerly awaiting my evening talk on poor and rich. These dedicated people jokingly continued, "You're going to solve all our problems." At the end of my presentation one person observed, "We came looking for answers, and you gave us more questions!" I replied that I had heard too many sad stories of experts descending upon a group and laying a trip on them like, "You people should give up your jobs and sell everything you own, so that you can truly follow the Gospel of the poor Jesus who had nowhere to lay his head."

In this chapter I do not plan to lay any trips on you. I want to guide you through data of a highly complex nature. We stop in four ports: (1) a definition of terms and a search for clarity; (2) biblical and extra-biblical traditions on poor and rich; (3) Luke's dreams for his communities; (4) Karris musings. From this last point you can see that I am not going to let myself off the hook of the question of the contemporary relevance of the Lukan theme of poor and rich. But I muse with you only after I have laid out the data. You can check my musings against that data. Further information can be found in my article, "Poor and Rich."

I. Definition of Terms
   and a Search for Clarity

Poor and rich are like community and love. Each person has his or her own definition of these popular terms. In support of my observation, I invite you to engage in a little experiment. Take out a piece of paper and a pen. Write down the names of three people you think are poor, and then the names of three people you think are rich. Now check over your list. If you're like me, you may have included among the names of the rich people the name of a person who is economically quite poor. My "rich" person lacks money, but is rich in joy, vision, happiness and friends. Again assume the writer's position and fill in the blanks: a poor person earns $___ a year; a rich person earns $___ a year. My figures, off the top of my head, are $5,000 for a poor person and $100,000 for a rich person. If you're using this book in a discussion group, you might share your jottings with one another. Such comparisons will alert us to one fact: we have to be very careful in approaching the theme of poor and rich in Luke-Acts. We bring to that subject our multiple and diverse ideas of poor and rich.

Because poor and rich are ambiguous terms, I

will supply working definitions. Section II below will nuance these definitions. I espouse the definition of a poor person given by the French scholar A. George. His definition is long and descriptive and reflects the complexity of the biblical data: "In the biblical mind, the poor person is less one who is indigent and more one who is oppressed, an inferior or a lesser one. It is a social idea. This is why later, when the poor begin to spiritualize their condition, their ideal will not become detachment from the goods of this world but rather a voluntary and loving submission to the will of God" (*Gospel Poverty: Essays in Biblical Theology*. Chicago, 1977, p. 6). If we reverse George's definition of a poor person, we have our definition of a rich person. In brief, the rich are those who have considerable possessions or money or power or pride; they oppress. Sharing the common ground of these basic ideas, we can now approach the various traditions on the thematic of poor and rich.

II. Biblical and Extra-Biblical Traditions on Poor and Rich

A. The Old Testament

In this section my goal is to sensitize us to our tendency to harmonize the diverse traditions of the Old Testament, e.g., to try to explain away the condemnation of the poor person found in portions of the Wisdom literature. I also want to encourage us to strip off the commonly held, but faulty, developmental approach to the Old Testament whereby what is written last is assumed to be the culmination of all that has gone before. This is the approach to the theme of poor and rich popularized by A. Gelin's pathfinding *The Poor of Yahweh*. According to Gelin's developmental hypothesis, the peak of God's revelation on the theme of poverty in the Old Testament is the view of the poor person as the symbol of an attitude of dependence on God (see #5 below). Gelin reasons that Jesus is heir to this view of poverty. Thus Jesus' beatitudes deal with spiritual poverty and not with real poverty.

At the end of each delineation of five Old Testament traditions, I will hint at the connection between that particular tradition and Luke-Acts.

(1) To Be Poor Is a Punishment

The blessings promised in Deuteronomy single out wealth and plenty as a sign of God's blessings; to be poor is a curse. See, for example, Deuteronomy 28:12-13. Recall Luke 18:24-25: " 'For it is easier for a camel to go through the eye of a needle than for a rich man to enter the kingdom of God.' Those who heard it said, 'Then who can be saved?' " For these questioners, an individual's riches were a sign of God's favor.

2. Poverty Is a Scandal, a Breach of Covenant with God

During the time of Israel's kings, who, as God's vicars, were supposed to care for the widow, orphan, and poor, there was frequent breach of that charge. Some Israelites went against God's covenant and oppressed their fellow Israelites. The prophetic rail against this oppression of and assault on the poor is perhaps nowhere more forcefully expressed than in Amos 8:4-6. I would suggest reading Jesus' first beatitude against this backdrop: "Blessed are you poor, for yours is the kingdom of God" (Luke 6:20). God's reign, proclaimed by Jesus, is for the poor.

3. The Poor Man Is Poor Because He Is Lazy

In its typical style the Wisdom literature places contrary proverbs almost side by side. It praises and condemns both rich and poor. For our purposes it is important to listen attentively to passages like: "A slack hand causes poverty, but the hand of the diligent makes rich" (Proverbs 10:4; see also Proverbs 6:6-11). This tradition was much alive during Jesus' day. See Luke 16:14 and also our treatment on rabbinic thought.

4. The Religious Duty of Almsgiving

Deuteronomy 15:11 is one passage among

many which lays down the duty of almsgiving: "For the poor will never cease out of the land; therefore I command you, You shall open wide your hand to your brother, to the needy and to the poor, in the land." It seems that the rich man in Luke 16:19-31 neglected the duty of almsgiving, a duty which Jesus taught was still valid: "But it is easier for heaven and earth to pass away, than for one dot of the law to become void" (Luke 16:17).

5. The Poor Person Is a Symbol of a Spiritual Attitude toward God

In two of the latest prophetic sections of the Bible the poor person is a symbol for an open-handed attitude toward God, an attitude of total dependence. God rewards such an attitude. Isaiah 66:2 goes: "All these things my hand has made, and so all these things are mine, says the Lord. But this is the man to whom I will look, he that is *humble* and contrite in spirit, and trembles at my word." See also Zephaniah 3:12. You recall that A. Gelin used these passages as the foundation stones for his reconstruction of who the "poor" were in Jesus' ministry and teaching. But as we have now seen, these passages are merely one voice in the chorus of the Old Testament. See the section on Qumran below and Luke 1:46-55.

In summary, all five of these Old Testament traditions were alive and well when Luke-Acts was being composed.

B. Qumran, the Seers, the Rabbis

At the risk of obscuring the landscape with the dark clouds of brevity, I will mention a few quick points about three Jewish groups. These groups are evidence of how some Jews at Jesus' time interpreted the Old Testament traditions about poor and rich.

1. Qumran

These people lived near the Dead Sea from ca. 130 B.C. to A.D. 70 and protested the legitimacy of the priestly authorities in Jerusalem. They were prosperous and held all things in common. In their eyes they were the poor, that is, the humble ones who acknowledged their sinfulness and expected salvation from the grace of God.

2. The Seers

In Jesus' day most Palestinians were dominated by irreligious, foreign oppressors and weighed down by heavy taxes. It seemed that God had abandoned them, his people. In such a situation seers read the palms of the past, gazed into the future, and plotted the course of liberation. They often predicted a time of reversal, a time when the rich would be upended. (See, for example, chapter 97 of the apocalyptic book called I Enoch.) When

Jesus came on the Palestinian scene, it was a tinderbox, ready for revolution.

3. The Rabbis

The rabbis tried to balance as many of the Old Testament traditions as possible. Martin Hengel comments: "Jewish piety, which took its stamp from the message of the prophets and the social commandments of the Torah, did its utmost to eliminate or at least to alleviate the particularly abrupt contrast between the rich and poor in the Hellenistic Roman period" (*Property and Riches in the Early Church*. Philadelphia, 1974, p. 19). Hengel goes on to say: "Among the rabbis we increasingly find once again the high estimate put on riches and the despising of the poor which were characteristic of early wisdom" (p. 21). The rabbis did not chase after poverty, but tried to eliminate it. For them poverty was not a sign that one was near God.

In sum, at the time of Jesus there are various Old Testament traditions on poor and rich, plus Qumranites, who are prosperous, but who call themselves poor, who depend on God for life and forgiveness. There are oppressed communities, whose anguish is given voice by the seers who foresee the destruction of the rich oppressors. There are rabbis who strive to eliminate poverty, which they consider a curse. And into this flood of traditions steps Jesus.

C. *Jesus of Nazareth*

Luke inherited traditions of how Jesus related to the poor and rich. We examine these traditions briefly.

Jesus of Nazareth preached the kingdom of God and befriended the poor. This combination of kingdom of God and befriending of the poor goes back to the Old Testament tradition according to which the king, as God's vicar, was to care for the widow, orphan, and poor (see above). When Jesus proclaims that the kingdom of God is at hand and acts out its meaning by caring for the poor, he gives living witness to God who, as King, cares for and is compassionate to the poor. The poor are blessed because God is merciful, not because they are poor. Put another way, the poverty of the poor is not a requirement for piety. We can put this facet of Jesus' ministry in still another way. Jesus does not idealize the materially poor. Both the poor and the rich are called to conversion.

Two other points, quickly. Jesus associated freely with the rich. He enjoined almsgiving.

D. *Non-Jewish Greco-Roman Traditions*

In discussions of the theme of poor and rich, Jewish traditions are often the only voices heard. But there are other traditions, whose voices should be heard. I now invite up to the speaker's rostrum those traditions espoused by non-Jewish folk who

were brought up in the traditions of Greece and
Rome. Three of their traditions shed considerable
light on our subject. While there may be overlap
between these three traditions, each one is sufficiently distinct to merit separate consideration.
First, almsgiving is not known among the Greco-
Romans. Second, the Greco-Romans would not
come to the aid of a needy non-citizen. The well-
known "bread and circuses" were only for citizens.
Third, Greco-Romans would help a friend in need,
but only to collect IOU's against future contingen-
cies. In this connection, we should remember that
for the Greco-Romans a friend was almost a carbon
copy of oneself, someone who had the same talents,
likes, and social status.

In order to make these Greco-Roman traditions
more understandable, allow me to anticipate their
relevance to our interpretation of Luke-Acts. Just
think of the difficulty missionaries from Luke's
communities would have communicating Jesus'
tradition of care for the poor to Greco-Romans.
These people would have to retrain their eyes just to
be able to see the poor person who was not a friend.
And difficulties would be compounded if these missionaries would raise the issue of giving alms to the
poor person. Further, in Acts 2:42-47 and 4:32-35,
Luke uses Greco-Roman friendship terminology
to describe the early Christian community. These
early Christians from diverse social standings were
friends, "of one heart and soul," "having all things
in common." Luke describes the Christian communities this way, so that non-Jewish converts

could understand in their own terms what Christians were about.

After I had given my presentation on poor and rich in Luke-Acts at an institute, an American-born missionary approached me. He observed that what I had said about the conflict between the Jesus traditions and the Greco-Roman culture helped him understand a vital aspect of his work among an African tribe. He continued, "Now I know why one tribe will never accept someone in need from another tribe, no matter how hard I try to convince the chief. The chief repeats over and over, 'We cannot waste our resources on an outsider.' " Perhaps we need not go to Africa to find additional examples of needy persons who do not exist because they are not citizens or members of the family or club.

Now that we have primed the pump almost to the point of explosion with our many and diverse traditions on poor and rich, let's visit with Luke and ask him about his dreams for his communities.

III. Luke's Dreams for His Communities

If you are frustrated with the mass of traditions on poor and rich I have presented, welcome to the club. I have often been frustrated in my attempts and those of others to make sense of this plethora of data. But if I regard Luke, not as a linear thinker, but as a spherical one, I feel less frustrated. Recall what I mentioned in Chapter 1. Luke is a spherical thinker who knows that there are many ways of getting to the center of the sphere of poor and rich. We may also be helped in recalling that Luke may be likened to the overseer of missionary communities which are tributary to diverse traditions. Luke has not felt it his duty to suppress these traditions, but to incorporate them into his biblical history. In this regard, Luke could be profitably compared to a religious leader who encourages different ways of celebrating the Eucharist in missionary churches. In one the celebrant sits lotus style, in another she stands.

In this section I employ the imagery of "dreams" to imply that Luke has no ready-made answer to the problematic of poor and rich. Rather he dreams dreams, he projects a vision for his communities. I further imply that he often uses the theme of poor and rich in a symbolic way to accomplish his purposes of showing that the Christian community stands in continuity with Israel's finest traditions, of inspiring his communities with models from the past, and of encouraging his persecuted communities. In what follows we contemplate Luke's vision from these angles: almsgiving, models for Luke's communities, and the meaning of possessions.

A. Almsgiving

A careful reading of Luke-Acts or the diligent use of a concordance will reward one handsomely with the many passages which deal with almsgiving.

Here we can only touch on basic points. For Luke, almsgiving is not the quarter for a cup of coffee. It is symbolic of true adherence to the Old Testament Law. This point is so important that it bears repetition. Almsgiving must be seen in reference to the Old Testament Law.

Seen from this perspective, passages like Luke 11:41 and 16:14 leap alive with meaning. In 11:40-41 Jesus excoriates the Pharisees. They are to give alms, and then everything will be clean. Ritual cleanliness pales in the face of the obligation of almsgiving. In Luke 16:9-13 Jesus gives instructions about the duty of almsgiving. Luke observes in the very next verse: "The Pharisees, who were lovers of money, heard all this, and they scoffed at him" (Luke 16:14). It seems that Luke, with his theme of almsgiving, abets his purpose of writing Luke-Acts: Jesus and the communities which march under his colors stand in the finest tradition of Israel, are truly obedient to the Law, and enjoin almsgiving. They are not like the Pharisees, those leaders of Israel, who do not observe the commandment of almsgiving. In brief, almsgiving can function as a symbol of adherence to the Jewish Law and is not the simple doling out of a quarter or of last year's dress to someone in need.

Almsgiving also symbolizes conversion. On one level the stories found in Luke 18:18-30 and 19:1-10 are somewhat contradictory. The rich ruler is required to sell all, distribute to the poor, and then follow Jesus (18:22) whereas Zacchaeus gets off with giving a mere half of his goods to the poor (19:8). Whatever the solution may be to the problem of why one is required to give all and another to give only half, Luke requires that these men show the genuineness of their conversion by means of almsgiving. The test of genuine conversion is the person's willingness to move out of his or her own world to help those in need. And this process of moving out of the world of self is inspired by the Old Testament command of almsgiving.

In summary, as you read over other passages in Luke-Acts which deal with almsgiving, ask yourselves whether almsgiving may be symbolic of true adherence to the Old Testament Law and of conversion.

B. Models for Luke's Communities

In Chapters 2 and 3 we indicated that Luke's intention was to write the continuation of biblical history and that he was the first to author the lives of the saints. In this section we will see how these points interweave with the theme of poor and rich.

1. Jesus

Jesus of Nazareth befriended the poor because he was the ambassador, the agent of God's reign which was for the alleviation of poverty. This Jesus is the prime model for what Luke's communities should be about. All other traditions have to be filtered through the image of Jesus, friend of the poor. And if we look beyond the physical suffering of the poor to their powerlessness, we can begin to see how the theme of Jesus' table fellowship with the outcasts intersects with the theme of Jesus' care for the poor. Both outcasts and poor were powerless.

Luke interprets Jesus of Nazareth's actual ministry to the poor via his key theological insight of fulfillment of promise. See Chapter 4 above, especially on Luke 7:18-35. Luke 7:22 describes Jesus' ministry as a fulfillment of the promises of Isaiah the prophet: Jesus preaches good news to the poor. The community which follows Jesus will continue in word and deed his preaching of good news to the poor.

2. The Early Christian Community

By repeating the content of Acts 2:44-45 in Acts 4:32-34, Luke places great stress on the early Christian community's life of sharing. As we noted above, Luke uses the Greco-Roman terminology of friendship to help his non-Jewish readers appreciate the heart of Christian community—sharing of life together. But not only that—the early Christian community experienced the fulfillment of the Jewish longing for a land free from need (compare Acts 4:34 and Deuteronomy 15:4).

As is his literary wont, Luke does not think it
necessary to repeat these messages each time he
narrates the formation of a new Christian community. The sharing of goods among the first Christians and their experience of being free from need
are two of Luke's premiere dreams.

3. Peter

In the picture of Peter we linger on two points.
Peter is the model for a Church leader. He has no
silver and gold, but gives what he has. "In the name
of Jesus Christ of Nazareth, walk" (Acts 3:6). And
the cripple walks.

In Peter's confrontation with Simon Magus we
find a negative example (Acts 8:18-24). The impart-
ing of the Holy Spirit through the laying on of hands
is not for sale. Leaders in Luke's communities
should fashion their lives on that of Peter; money
did not erode his fidelity to God.

4. Cornelius

Acts 10:2 depicts Cornelius as "a devout man
who feared God with all his household, gave alms
liberally to the people, and prayed constantly to
God" (see also 10:4, 31). Cornelius, the first Gentile
convert, observes the Jewish Law of almsgiving
and is ripe for the Holy Spirit's call. While Luke

might have used other means of describing Cornelius, he chose and repeated the picture of almsgiver. Cornelius is a hero for those non-Jews who find it difficult to give alms. Cornelius was rewarded generously by God for his almsgiving.

5. *Paul*

Luke underscores Paul's Jewishness by means of the theme of almsgiving. See Acts 24:17: "Now after some years I came (to Jerusalem) to bring to my nation alms and offerings." Through his observance of this key point of Jewish Law, Paul stands in continuity with the twelve apostles, who stand in continuity with Jesus, who is the fulfillment of God's promises of old.

Paul is also the patron saint of ministers. In his farewell speech to the Ephesian elders Paul selects this feature from his ministry: "I coveted no one's silver or gold or apparel. You yourselves know that these hands ministered to my necessities, and to those who were with me. In all things I have shown you that by so toiling one must help the weak, remembering the words of the Lord Jesus, how he said, 'It is more blessed to give than to receive' " (Acts 20:33-35). In his ministry Paul uses a word of Jesus as a beacon and thus lights the way for those who minister in his footsteps.

As we glance once more at the gallery of Lukan models, we note these characteristics. In imitation of Jesus, Christians minister to the powerless. In imitation of Peter and Paul, Christian ministers do not use their ministry for self-aggrandizement. In imitation of the first Christian communities, Christians share with one another so that no one is in need.

C. The Meaning of Possessions

At the outset let me state explicitly something that has been implied in much of what I have said so far in this chapter. The Lukan communities contained members who had possessions. They may not have been patricians in the Roman social pecking order. Perhaps, they were freedmen, who had purchased their freedom, were socially mobile, and were rapidly accumulating wealth. In any case, some people within the Lukan communities had sufficient possessions to fall within the category of rich. At the risk of overstating the obvious, let me put the matter a little differently. Our commonly held images of the first Christians as poor slaves and ignoramuses are inaccurate. A significant number of Luke's Christians were rich and educated.

And the wealth of Christians within Luke's communities could get them into trouble when the pollution of persecution filled the air. To continue his walk with Jesus, a Christian freedman might have to turn his back on his possessions and all the things he had come to value as signs of his freedom. To these people Luke offers a challenge and a model. His challenge is found in Luke 14:33, which

I could paraphrase this way: "In a persecution situation when it's Jesus or your possessions, renounce all your possessions and fall in line behind Jesus." The model is found in the person of the Thessalonian Christian named Jason. This convert of some few days perseveres in a persecution situation even though he has to put his possessions on the block by going bond/security for himself and others (Acts 17:9).

And the possessions of Christians cannot be interpreted as an unconditional sign of God's favor. The God of Surprises evokes the gasp of "Then who can be saved?" (Luke 18:26) when Jesus announces that it is difficult for the rich ruler to enter the kingdom of God. A similar surprise seems to be behind Luke 16:27-31: What's such a nice rich person like you doing in such a place of torment? Isn't wealth a sign of blessing? The rich man's five brothers have Moses and the prophets who enjoin God's law of almsgiving. Let them heed their message.

At the end of this section we spot the trail of our theme of The Faithful God. Three passages in particular point us to that trail: "A man's life does not consist in the abundance of his possessions" (Luke 12:15); "For where your treasure is, there will your heart be also" (Luke 12:34); "You cannot serve God and mammon" (Luke 16:13). To hold onto one's possessions for dear life is to lose hope in God, to close one's hands around goods rather than to hold them open in dependence on God. Possessions are not evil in themselves. It's we who turn them into gods, it's we who measure our worth by them, it's we who wrap our hearts around them. We define ourselves by our possessions, our virtues, our accomplishments, our "this," our "that." What I am groping to express here has been articulated most vigorously by the philosopher Gabriel Marcel when he meditates on hope and possessions: "What, however, we might perhaps dare to say is that if, however feebly, we remain penetrated by hope, it can only be through the cracks and openings which are to be found in the armour of Having which covers us: the armour of our possessions, our attainments, our experiences and our virtues, perhaps even more than our vices" (*Homo Viator*. N.Y., 1951, p. 62).

IV. Karris Musings

We have completed our task of laying out the data on the theme of poor and rich. Allow me to present some of my dreaming about Luke's dreams. Or to change the image, let me share some visions with you. Perhaps you will find looking at the theme of poor and rich through my eyes congenial and challenging.

Poverty is an evil which is to be stamped out. The kingdom of God which Jesus brings is a frontal attack on the evil by which people are made and kept economically poor and oppressed. It seems to me that spiritual writers and popular preachers do a disservice to the Christian community and to humanity in general when they glorify poverty. The

Gospel by its very nature is social, a point missed by those who want to keep the Christian community and its ministers in the sacristy and away from demonstrations for human rights. Salvation is for the total human person, not just for some disembodied soul.

The early Christian community of Acts 2 and 4 is presented as a model because of its sharing with those in need and not because of its "poverty." From these two texts I have been learning the additional lesson of hospitality, of welcoming others into my heart and home. From these texts I have also been learning the lesson of the necessity of translating the Christian message into the language of another culture.

These days the biggest lesson I am learning is that I must appear before my Faithful God with open hands. While I know that I cannot take anything with me, I keep a knapsack of virtues at the ready, on my back. I'm also prepared to check every entry of the recording angel against the tally sheet I keep of my accomplishments.

As you come to the end of this chapter, I hope that you can say that I haven't laid a trip on you. I have blazed a trail for you and for myself through the territory of the Lukan theme of poor and rich. I have drawn much refreshment and inspiration from preparing this trail with you. I invite you to travel it again and again, stopping from time to time to capture the beauty of each vista. Be my guest.

8
Spirit, Fidelity,
Continuity, and Community

As I come to the end of this book, some of my readers might well chide me, "It's about time you treated the Spirit. Since grade school I've heard that the Acts of the Apostles is the Gospel of the Holy Spirit. And you've left the Spirit to last." "With the charismatic movement bursting out all over these days, why did you wait till the end to share your insights on the Spirit?" I agree that the Holy Spirit rates high in Luke's theology, but I have waited until now so that I could put Luke's treatment of the Spirit in a broader context. That broader context is the entire book of Luke-Acts; it is also the God who is faithful to promise; it is Jesus who receives the promised Holy Spirit from the Father; it is Luke's communities who explain to themselves and others how they stand in continuity with those who have received God's Spirit in the past. In a sense, then, this chapter summarizes previous themes from a fresh perspective.

In sections I, II, and III continuity will be the password. Section IV broaches contemporary charismatic issues. I conclude with a crop of Karris musings.

I. *The Spirit and Fulfillment of Promise*

The Spirit is present during the events of the Infancy Narrative, during Jesus' ministry, and at the birth of the Church. Luke interprets these three cardinal events by means of his thematic of fulfillment of promise.

A. *Luke's Infancy Narrative*

Luke 1:5—2:52 is replete with references to the Spirit, especially the Spirit of prophecy. For example, it is said of Zechariah, John the Baptist's father, that he "was filled with the Holy Spirit, and prophesied" (1:67); moreover, Anna is a prophetess (2:36). In order to understand fully what Luke has in mind in these opening chapters, we should fashion clear ideas on two points. First, the prime meaning of "to prophesy" is to forth-tell. That is, the prophet is the one who tells forth God's will. Only secondarily does the prophet foretell the future. Point two is that at the time of Jesus' birth it was commonly hoped that an outpouring of God's Spirit would accompany the coming of the Messiah.

The meaning of Jesus' birth is forth-told by the various prophetic voices in Luke 1:5—2:52. God has fulfilled his promises in Jesus. In the events surrounding the birth of the Messiah, Jesus, God's Spirit has been poured forth.

One final, but vital note. The prophetic words of Luke 1:5—2:52 are directional signs of what is to follow. The announcement that God has fulfilled his promise in Jesus contains within itself the seeds of another promise. Let me illustrate my point with a recent experience.

Experiencing God's fulfillment of promise can be likened to the experience I had of being given a tour of a person's home. As I was ushered into the first room on the tour, I was almost swept off my feet. The colors, the patterns, the furniture, the carpet—all blended together to create a visual experience of great beauty and delight. As the hostess was escorting me to other rooms in the house, I anticipated the same extraordinary experience. That one experience had shown me so much of the hostess' good taste and artistry that I "knew" that each new room on the tour would be a masterpiece and a delight. If questioned, I could give no proof for my "knowledge" that each additional room on the tour would be a work of art. On the basis of one experience I simply knew in anticipation that it would be so. And I was not disappointed. We expect that the God who took our breath away with one fulfillment of promise will continue to delightfully surprise us. In that fulfillment of promise he sowed seeds of promise which blossom and bear fruit.

Lest I leave Luke 1:5—2:52 in the dust as I scurry off to find further contemporary illustrations, I conclude this section with a reference to Simeon upon whom the Holy Spirit rested (2:25). Of Jesus Simeon prophesies: "Mine eyes have seen thy salvation which thou hast prepared in the presence of all peoples, a light for revelation to the Gentiles, and for glory to thy people Israel. . . . Behold, this child is set for the fall and rising of many in Israel, and for a sign that is spoken against" (Luke 2:30-32, 34). Simeon forth-tells that Jesus is God's salvation for both Jew and Gentile, and then opens up the future and gives glimpses of Jesus' checkered life of acceptance and rejection.

In brief, God fulfills his promise of giving the Holy Spirit by gracing the hope-filled people of the Infancy Narrative. God is The Faithful God.

B. Jesus

Since I have dedicated an entire chapter to this theme and will be devoting some space to it in section II below, I will keep my remarks here to a minimum. For Luke, Jesus is the man of the Spirit par excellence. Luke leaves no doubt that the Holy Spirit descended upon Jesus at his baptism, for he alone says: "The Holy Spirit descended upon him *in bodily form*, as a dove" (Luke 3:22). "In bodily form" means "really," "essentially." Peter preaches to Cornelius that God was with Jesus because Jesus was anointed with the Holy Spirit: "God anointed Jesus of Nazareth with the Holy Spirit and with power; he went about doing good and healing all that were oppressed by the devil, for God was with him" (Acts 10:38).

But the attention-arresting factor in Luke's presentation of Jesus' anointing by the Spirit is that this anointing was in fulfillment of promise. Recall Jesus' inaugural sermon at Nazareth wherein he announces that he fulfills what the Lord had promised through Isaiah: "The Spirit of the Lord is upon me" (see Luke 4:18, 21). Jesus is the man of the Spirit par excellence because God is faithful to his promises.

C. The Church

It is often remarked that Pentecost is the birth of the Church, and that statement is true as far as it goes. But there would be no Pentecost and no Church unless the Father were faithful to his promises. Jesus tells his disciples: "And behold, I send *the promise of my Father* upon you; but stay in the city, until you are clothed with power from on high" (Luke 24:49). And a key verse in Peter's sermon, which interprets the event of Pentecost, runs: "Being therefore exalted at the right hand of God, and having received *from the Father the promise of the Holy Spirit*, he has poured out this which you see and hear" (Acts 2:33).

In sum, Luke integrates the gift of the Holy Spirit into his theology of The Faithful God who fulfills his promises. The Faithful God of Israel again breathes forth his Spirit—on the hope-filled

Simeon and companions, on Jesus, and on the Church.

II. Jesus and Other Men of the Spirit

Luke uses the theme of the Spirit to show continuity between Jesus, the man of the Spirit par excellence, and the leaders of the early Christian communities. These leaders are Peter, the twelve apostles, Stephen, Philip, Barnabas and Paul. Each one is described as filled with the Holy Spirit. In Jesus' stead these men of the Spirit preach, work signs and wonders, and are met with acceptance and rejection—a description very similar to that given of Jesus in Acts 2:22 and 10:35 and found in narrative form in the Gospel of Luke.

These men of the Spirit not only continue the ministry of Jesus, they also replace the leaders of Israel. Those who reject the preaching of these leaders cut themselves off from the Israel of the promises.

In summary, Luke uses the concept of the prophetic Spirit to show continuity between Jesus and the new leaders of Israel. (See Johnson, pp. 29-78 for more detail on this point.)

III. Beginnings and Endings

From the perspective of the theme of the Holy

Spirit, let's retrace the steps we took in Chapter 2. Additional insights await us.

A. *Luke 1—2 and Acts 1—2*

Luke has gone out of his way to parallel the beginnings of the two parts of his one-volume work. In both of these beginnings we find people waiting in prayer for the fulfillment of God's promises. In each case the fulfillment of God's promise is the gift of the Holy Spirit. In both instances that fulfillment of promise opens up the door to another promise. Luke 1—2 opens up on the life of Jesus; Acts 1—2 opens up on the life of the Christian community. Luke's patterning of these two beginnings is not just due to literary skill. On a theological level he is saying that the Spirit is God's agent of fulfillment of promise, that the Spirit is creative Spirit.

B. *Luke 24:49 and Acts 28*

The Gospel ends with the disciples leaning forward toward the gift of the Spirit: "Behold, I send the promise of my Father upon you; but stay in the city, until you are clothed with power from on high" (Luke 24:49). This promise is fulfilled in the event of Pentecost, which forms the beginning of Acts.

Ostensibly Luke-Acts ends without a reference

to the Holy Spirit. As a matter of fact, references to the Spirit are scarce in the last thirteen chapters of Acts. But this phenomenon should not startle us, for Luke has a different purpose in these last chapters, namely, to prove the Jewishness of Paul, the hero of his missionary communities. When Paul reaches Rome in Acts 28, Luke does not mean to say that missionary activity to either Jew or Gentile has ceased (see Chapters 2 and 3). This missionary activity still pulses in the lives of Luke's missionaries who witness to Jesus in the power of the Spirit (see Acts 1:8) and who pattern their missionary work after that of Paul (see Chapters 2 and 3). Acts 16:6-7 provides a resume of how the Spirit directed the missionary activity of the model missionary, Paul: "And they (Paul and Timothy) went through the region of Phrygia and Galatia, having been forbidden by the Holy Spirit to speak the word in Asia. And when they had come opposite Mysia, they attempted to go into Bithynia, but the Spirit of Jesus did not allow them."

In brief, reflection upon the theme of the Spirit in conjunction with beginnings and endings may help us solve a problem which has baffled scholars for years: How can one call Acts the Gospel of the Holy Spirit when that main character is absent from so many of the last chapters of Acts? That main character, the Spirit, is present in the life of Paul, directing him on mission. Luke encourages his missionary communities with the assurance that the Spirit is with them, too, on mission.

IV. Contemporary Issues—Spirit and Community

It is not possible to treat all the contemporary charismatic issues, nor to handle in great detail those I discuss. An orientation tour of the issues will have to suffice.

A. Spirit Creates Community and Impels to Mission

A careful reading of Acts 1—2 indicates that the Spirit creates community. It is not just the twelve apostles, but all 120 gathered in prayer who receive the Holy Spirit at Pentecost. The number 120 is suggestive of the formation of a new community, for rabbinic law has it that 120 inhabitants are necessary for a town to have a small sanhedrin. And Mary and other women are members of this new community, created by the Spirit. And since 3,000 repentant Jews join this community, it an be called the restored Israel, those whom God has restored to faithful adherence to his word (Acts 2:41).

The Spirit impels this community to mission. The list of all known nations in Acts 2:8-11 points to worldwide mission. The inspirited apostles do not turn in upon themselves, but engage in the missionary activity of telling everyone about "the mighty works of God" (Acts 2:11). We will have more to say about Spirit and mission in part C below.

B. *The Spirit and Prayer*

In Chapter 6 I called your attention to Luke 11:13 where Luke alone says that the Father will give the Holy Spirit to those who ask him in prayer. In Acts 4:24-31, a passage often termed "The Little Pentecost," Luke presents us with a narrative of how God answers prayer with the gift of the Holy Spirit: "And when they had prayed, the place in which they were gathered together was shaken; and they were all filled with the Holy Spirit and spoke the word of God with boldness" (Acts 4:31). In this passage we have another instance in which Luke links the Spirit and mission. The Spirit enables the community to go forth, in a persecution situation, and speak the word of God with boldness.

C. *Speaking in Tongues—Glossolalia*

I submit that Luke details three manifestations of the Holy Spirit: (1) a gift given to every Christian at baptism, e.g., Acts 2:38; (2) an endowment for select individuals, e.g., the men of the Spirit like Peter (see section II above); (3) a guide for the Church on mission, e.g., Acts 16:6-7. The phenomenon of speaking in tongues or glossolalia falls under the third type of manifestation. It is a visible, external sign that the Holy Spirit has ratified missionary expansion. This opinion needs clarification, so let's look at Acts 8:18, 10:44-46 and 19:6—the places where speaking in tongues occurs.

Relative to Acts 8:18, Simon Magus could only see that the Samaritans had received the gift of the Spirit if there were some external, visible sign of that gifting. The parallel passage in Acts 10:44-46 intimates that that external manifestation was the phenomenon of speaking in tongues: "While Peter was still saying this, the Holy Spirit fell on all who heard the word. And the believers from among the circumcised who came with Peter were amazed, because the gift of the Holy Spirit had been poured out even on the Gentiles. For they heard them speaking in tongues and extolling God." Acts 19:6 forms another parallel passage, for in that passage the Spirit ratifies Paul's missionary activity among the disciples of John the Baptist through the external manifestation of the Spirit's gift of speaking in tongues.

We can approach the glossolalia mentioned in Acts 8:18, 10:44-46 and 19:6 from another angle. If we agree that Luke uses the phenomenon of speaking in tongues as a way of showing that the Spirit ratifies missionary activity among certain people, then we can shed the clumsy clothes of problems like: "Why couldn't Philip impart the Holy Spirit to the Samaritans? Is Acts 8:14-17 the biblical basis for the sacrament of confirmation? How could Cornelius and his household receive the Holy Spirit without first receiving baptism? Luke uses the phenomenon of speaking in tongues as an external sign of the Spirit's ratification of the Church's move into a new missionary phase. Recall that Acts 8:14-18 occurs in the context of the Gospel moving into the territory of the Samaritans, that Acts 10:44-46 occurs in the context of the missionary expansion to pagans in the person of Cornelius, and that Acts 19:6 concerns missionary activity among a "fringe group," the disciples of John the Baptist. Through glossolalia the Spirit gives notice to all that he puts his stamp of approval on these missionary endeavors.

In summary, Luke does not examine the phenomenon of speaking in tongues for its own sake or for the sake of its recipients. His concern is not that of Paul in 1 Corinthians 12—14: the relationship of the gifts of the Spirit to the body of Christ. Luke uses glossolalia to further his theme of missionary expansion.

V. Karris Musings

Section IV above contained many of my musings. Here I expand some of those reflections and add new ones.

Luke does not reflect on the Holy Spirit in the same way that Paul or John do. Luke highlights the connection between the Spirit and mission. The Spirit, indeed, is the presence of the risen Lord Jesus in the community. The Spirit guides and directs (see Acts 15:28). But the Spirit is primarily for mission.

The Spirit is the supreme surpriser. The persecuted of Luke's communities are prepared to be surprised many times: "And when they bring you before the synagogues and the rulers and the authorities, do not be anxious how or what you are to answer or what you are to say; for the Holy Spirit will teach you in that very hour what you ought to say" (Luke 12:11-12). Like the brilliant apologies of the imprisoned Paul, the apologies of the persecuted in Luke's communities are born of the Holy Spirit (see Acts 21—26). Missionaries may have plotted their strategy and may think that they know where they are going, what they are going to do, and how. But the Spirit has other plans, as the story of Peter's Spirit-directed mission to Cornelius amply illustrates.

Personally, I think that the Spirit is at his surprising best in answer to prayer. In prayer I search and knock, and seem to unearth nothing, to find no one at home. Then suddenly the Spirit opens my heart to see the Father's handiwork in my life. Flashes of light illumine the paths of my past, so that I can walk them in the present, and detect directions for future travel. The more I come to prayer with open hands, the more I am surprised and delighted. Maybe it's because at forty I have enough life behind me to see patterns; maybe it's because at forty I realize more fully and clearly for whom and for what I am willing to die. But with that thought we have taken our first step along the road of the final chapter, to which we now turn.

9
Summary and
Luke's Vision

Last summer I took a ten-day guided tour of Israel. At the end of each day I made an entry into my diary. I recorded the jokes and interesting points made by the guide, but devoted the lion's share of each day's entry to my own reflections upon what we had seen. As we come to the end of this guided tour of Luke-Acts, this tour guide opens his diary and shares with you some additional reflections on the themes we have experienced together.

I. My View and Previous
Scholarship on Luke-Acts

For those who are using this book as a textbook or in connection with a course on Luke-Acts, it may be helpful if I would chart my position on the scholarly map of Luke-Acts. My position stands in line with the Yale professors—Paul Schubert, Paul

Minear, Nils Dahl, and Luke Johnson—who view Luke-Acts from the perspective of promise and fulfillment. My perspective meshes well with that of Frederick Danker, for whom Luke's theme is: "God, the Great Benefactor, reaches out to his world at the time appointed through his rejected Servant-Benefactor Jesus and through his Benefactor-Servant-Community, Israel-the-Church" (p. 104). To Jacques Dupont I owe a huge debt of gratitude for opening my eyes to the significance of mission in Luke-Acts.

While very appreciative of the outstanding contributions Hans Conzelmann has made to Lukan studies, I must demur from his position that Luke's primary concern was the delay of the parousia and that Luke substituted for eschatology a tripartite view of salvation history. Charles H. Talbert has been influential in my thinking, but I do not think that Luke-Acts can be sufficiently explained from the background of a polemic against Gnostic heretics. For a more detailed scholarly map, see my "Missionary Communities."

As I mentioned in my Introduction, the motive force for my reflections on Luke-Acts has come from a source other than the scholarly guild. In wrestling with the question of tragic death, I have been put on one of Luke's wavelengths and empowered to forge a theology of Luke-Acts. This theology is not merely descriptive of what Luke was about, but has also been refined in the fire of my own life.

II. *Theology of Fulfillment of Promise*

Some time back I was catching a quick lunch by myself in a restaurant. Seated almost on top of two elderly ladies, I couldn't help but overhear their conversation. "Ethel, she called me a liar!" one lady moaned. She continued, "I haven't had anything to do with her since then." Her companion seemed a bit annoyed and tried to change the topic of conversation, "Hazel, this sure is a tasty sandwich." But Hazel was not easily sidetracked, "She called me a liar when I had gotten out of my bed of agony to greet her on her birthday." Almost in desperation Ethel rasped, "Hazel, this is all you ever talk about. Why do you punish yourself this way? After all, that happened fifty years ago!"

The misery of memory. If our memories are like Hazel's, then we are not going to be alive to the present. We live in the past, moribund. People could say of us, "I wonder what they did when they were still alive."

But there's also the joy of memory. Luke's theology of fulfillment of promise has taught me to view the past with gratitude. As I view the past with gratitude, I am open to the winds the Spirit sends my way in the present. I know that the God who has been faithful in the past will be faithful in the present. His fidelity generates mine. From his past action, which I view with gratitude, I am able to discern his present action and walk into the future with joy and confidence. Even the experience or anticipation of pain has lost part of its sting. I strive to be surprised by The Faithful God.

III. *Prayer*

Prayer is throwaway time in the presence of a loving Father. It is a search to see patterns in God's actions in the past—in my own life, in the lives of the members of my community, in the lives of the saints, in the lives of the people of the Bible. The Faithful God may be a God of Surprises, but he often surprises in a consistent way. Prayer allows me the time to seek out the consistency of God's patterns. From my present experience I probe the past and gaze into the future.

In the area of prayer I would like to develop the posture and outlook I have developed in viewing Peter Sellers in the Pink Panther movies. I have come to expect the surprises of misdirection, mis-identity, etc., to such an extent that often I am laughing seconds before the actual comic scene unfolds. While this skill runs me the risk of being thrown out of a movie theatre as a nuisance, I want to develop something similar to it in my search for God. Flexibility is the word for this forty-year-old.

IV. *Jesus*

In treating of Jesus, I have tried to give voice to

an aspect of Luke's view of Jesus which is often neglected in scholarly circles and which has been a powerful influence on my life. For Luke, Jesus was the outcast who hoped in the faithfulness of God, who is Father. This Jesus, who came for the poor and who celebrated table fellowship with sinners and outcasts, was condemned by the highest religious and civil authorities of his day as detrimental to the goals of religion and society. In this situation of utter rejection Jesus forgives, is true to his ministry to the outcasts, and prays "Father, into your hands I commit my spirit." The Faithful Father raised this Jesus who hoped against hope. In the name of this Jesus there is salvation. It is this Jesus who is Son of God. It is this Jesus who is present in the Christian community's breaking of bread.

V. *The Holy Spirit*

I know that the Father is faithful to his promises and I know that Jesus is faithful to his promises because I have experienced their Spirit. The presence of the Spirit is the concrete sign of the fidelity of Father and Son. The spirit illumines my past and present, and guides, nay, impels, me into the future. I must declare to others "the mighty works of the Lord." Like Jesus, I must befriend the outcasts and preach good news to the poor.

VI. Community

The diary notes I have shared in the previous sections have necessarily been heavy on "I," "me," and "mine." That's the style of diary. But in this section let me step outside the framework of the diary and briefly probe that factor which makes my diary writing possible. I refer to the experience of Christian community.

Jesus' gift of the Spirit at Pentecost formed the 120 into the first Christian community. This community sustained its life together by common prayer, by the breaking of bread, and by sharing its goods with those in need. By its mission to both Jew and non-Jew it fulfilled the Scripture promise that the Messiah was for all.

Moving away from the Lukan theme of Christian community and toward my home base, I maintain that my experience of Christian community has effected hope in me. I have been loved by members of my Christian community, who in loving me have reflected the Father's love, affirmed his life in me, and breathed hope into my being.

VII. The Faithful God

As you must know by now, the theme of The Faithful God has primacy of position on my sphere of Luke's theology. I conclude this book with further reflections on The Faithful God.

In earlier chapters I explored, from many angles, Luke's purpose for writing Luke-Acts, and so have no need to rehearse those explorations here. But it is necessary to mention one more point. Like the biblical historians before him, Luke wrote the continuation of God's dealings with his people as a confession of faith. Through the biblical history of Luke-Acts Luke praises God and invites his readers to praise the God who is faithful to promise. Small wonder, then, that songs of praise and exclamations of joy populate Luke-Acts and celebrate what a loving, faithful Father has done.

The joy expressed by the characters of Luke-Acts is like the joy you experience in the presence of a loved one when you feel that your heart is going to burst through the seams of your being. It's the joy of being forgiven and restored to friendship. It's the joy of being affirmed by an unexpected invitation to table fellowship. It's the joy of experiencing a promise being fulfilled. It's the joy of experiencing persecution for the name of Jesus. It's the joy of hearing God say to you that it is good that you are, that it is wonderful that you are.

In a world which men call mean and nasty, in a world where life can appear tough and cruel, in a world where to share oneself is to expose one's jugular vein, Luke celebrates life, community, and the goodness and fidelity of God, and he invites endless curtain calls for Jesus, the person of hope. He gives a vision for the future by using the past to illumine the contours of the present.

At this point prose fails me. I end by sharing with you a poem which has been aborning in me these weeks and months as I pondered The Faithful God of Luke-Acts.

HOPE IS . . .

Hope is a traffic jam, sleepless nights.
　　The cripple cheered the dawn and danced to the
　　song of life.

Hope is the betrayal of the citadel of self.
　　We hugged, we sobbed, we sought, we fought, we
　　grew and grew.

Hope is smog in our air, muggers on our streets,
　　wails of "No one cares!"
　　Smiles frolicked on the faces of the elderly as the
　　child skipped by.

Hope is the artist's brush, the composer's pen, the
　　presence of a friend.
　　The autumnal splendor slowed her pace and on
　　her face traced wonder.

Hope is horizon seen, dream dreamt, sunset-
　　sunrise.
　　The child snuggled up in his father's lap and slept.

Hope is offspring of love's embrace, life coiled and
　　thrust into the future.

Hope is Jesus praying "Father, into your hands I commit my spirit."

Selected Bibliography

Conzelmann, Hans. *The Theology of St. Luke.* N.Y., 1960.

Dahl, Nils A. "The Story of Abraham in Luke-Acts," *Studies in Luke-Acts.* Eds. L. E. Keck and J. L. Martyn. Nashville, 1966, pp. 139-158.

Danker, Frederick W. *Luke.* Philadelphia, 1976.

Dupont, Jacques. *Salvation to the Gentiles.* N.Y., 1979.

Haenchen, Ernst. *The Acts of the Apostles: A Commentary.* Philadelphia, 1971.

Jervell, Jacob. *Luke and the People of God.* Minneapolis, 1972.

Johnson, Luke T. *The Literary Function of Possessions in Luke-Acts.* Missoula, 1977.

Karris, Robert J. *Gospel of St. Luke.* Chicago, 1974.

———. *Invitation to Acts.* Garden City, 1978.

———. *Invitation to Luke.* Garden City, 1977.

———. "Missionary Communities: A New Paradigm for the Study of Luke-Acts," *Catholic Biblical Quarterly* 41 (1979).

———. "Poor and Rich: The Lukan Sitz im Leben," *Perspectives on Luke-Acts.* Ed. C. H. Talbert. Association of Baptist Professors of Religion, 1978, pp. 112-125. An earlier version of this article is available in *Society of Biblical Literature 1976 Seminar Papers*. Ed. G. MacRae. Missoula, 1976, pp. 219-233.

Minear, Paul S. "Luke's Use of the Birth Stories," *Studies in Luke-Acts*, pp. 111-130.

Schubert, Paul. "The Structure and Significance of Luke 24," *Neutestamentliche Studien für Rudolf Bultmann*. Berlin, 1954, pp. 165-186.

Talbert, Charles H. *Literary Patterns, Theological Themes and the Genre of Luke-Acts*. Missoula, 1974.

———. *Luke and the Gnostics*. Nashville, 1966.